The floral design above each chapter heading is from a petite-point crochet by Violette de Mazia from the collection of Hope Broker.

Dedicated to the teachers and students past,
present and future at the Barnes Foundation

REMEMBERING VIO

Violette de Mazia

DIRECTOR OF EDUCATION
AND
SPIRIT OF THE BARNES FOUNDATION

SERENA SHANKEN SKWERSKY, Ph.D.

Copyright © 2019 by Serena Shanken Skwersky
Philadelphia, PA.

Cover Photo: Violette is from the Collection of Bob and Sandy London

Cover and book design by Phil Wolfe of Phil Wolfe Graphic Design.

Kopel Publishing for the Department of Education at the Barnes Foundation

Table of Contents

1. Introduction vi
2. A Young Artist Meets Violette 1
3. Cimetière du Montparnasse 5
4. Rue Chaptal in Levallois-Perret 7
5. St. Gilles 9
6. Isabelle Gatti de Gamond 11
7. Fleeing to England 13
8. Boundary Road in St. John's Wood 15
9. The Love of Two Brothers 17
10. Absence Is to Love What Fire Is to the Wind 22
11. Crossing the Sea 42
12. All Clustered in One Violette 53
13. A Voice Akin to a Musical Instrument 67
14. Orchestrating Her Classes 70
15. A Melina Mercouri, a Fifi D'Orsay 75
16. A Leavening Sensibility 81
17. Ebbing Away, Yet Writing Away 100
18. The Mantra and Her Legacy 108
19. Epilogue 111

v

Introduction

Violette de Mazia saw me sketching in the gallery that fall day in 1962. She walked in with a certain speed that seemed to say she knew I was there. With a quick, though studied, glance, Violette assessed my eighteen-year-old self. She paused. Was Violette remembering herself as an eighteen-year-old when she was still a student learning English and might have spent her leisure hours sketching at the British Museum? She was a recent émigré to London from France during the First World War. Did she see a little of herself in me? Whatever her measure, she saw no harm and let me be. Powerfully silent, she spoke tomes with her weighted look, scanning my body language and judging its intent. The image of her in that moment has stayed with me through all these years, but she is no longer silent. She speaks to me now through her essays, her letters, and her teachings; and I am now writing my response.

A Young Artist Meets Violette

One day in 1959, a teenage boy who aspired to become an artist decided to "go see the pictures" at the Barnes Foundation. Traveling from South Philadelphia was a long trek, and he was unsure of how to get to the Barnes. After looking at a map, figuring out which buses and trolleys to take, then taking the wrong ones and having to backtrack, he ended up at the Lord & Taylor department store on City Line Avenue. From there, he headed toward St. Joseph's University but failed to make a right at 54th Street.

As the boy continued, he ran into a priest who knew about the Barnes Foundation and directed him to Lapsley Lane, a short block that comes to a dead end and curves right into Latches Lane. There at the end of the lane was a huge iron fence that had a chain and a lock on it. Looking through it, the boy saw lights on in the Foundation and climbed over the gate, walked up to the monumental entrance, and knocked on the door. A little woman with dark glasses and semicurly hair that had a big flower in it opened the door and in absolute shock asked him who he was, what he was doing there, and how he got there. The young boy responded that he'd come a long way, climbed over the gate, and knocked on the door. "Well, you go away," she said. He told her he had come to see the paintings. "Wasn't it a museum," he asked?

And she said, "No." "Wasn't this the Barnes?" "Yes," she replied. Then this was the place where he wanted to be. Again she said, "No, go away."

But he'd traveled a long distance and asked if he could have a glass of water before he left. She looked at the teenaged boy very hard and said, "Okay, come in, but wait here in the vestibule." She went to get him the glass of water; but instead of waiting, the boy went into the gallery and saw the big Picasso and the Matisse mural and then wandered farther into the gallery and was just in awe, completely dumbstruck. First there was the huge Cezanne, then the Seurat…. He looked around at all the other paintings and saw the entrances to other galleries.

And the boy didn't realize it, but the woman was standing there with a glass of water watching him. She came over and started to talk to him. He was very taken with the Seurat; it was the first thing he fell in love with there. And he and the woman started to talk about it. Then the boy looked at the big Cezanne, *The Card Players,* and they started to talk about that. The boy even told the woman that the little Cezanne next to *The Card Players*—*Leda and the Swan*—was not a very good painting, and that the big Cezanne needed something better. She laughed. Then they walked through the galleries together and talked and talked for almost two hours, just the young boy, the sole visitor in the gallery, and this woman, guiding him through.

Soon the boy discovered that the woman was Violette de Mazia and that she knew his high school art teacher and the teacher's wife. Both had attended the Barnes Foundation and knew her well.[1] This helped Violette to trust him. She gave him directions to get back to his home, and the trip that took him nearly four hours from his home to Latches Lane took him barely an hour on his return.

On Monday morning, back at school, the boy's art teacher said that he'd heard the boy had been to the Barnes and that he was very anxious to know what he thought. Thereafter, the young boy, Peter Paone, spent many lunch hours in the art room, where he and his teacher would sit and talk about the Barnes. About two months after Peter's jaunt to Latches Lane, his art teacher asked him if he'd like to attend the Barnes: Violette de Mazia invited him to be in her class.

As a student at the Barnes, Peter sat in the front row. The class was small, with only twenty people, so they were able to sit in folding chairs that they moved from gallery to gallery and to pass around small original works by Picasso and Toulouse-Lautrec during the lectures. For Peter, the beauty of sitting in the Barnes for three-hour lectures was just being in the rooms full of paintings.

During Peter's high school years, when he was living with his parents on Seventh and Dickinson Street, in South Philadelphia, Violette visited his home, where he had a small basement studio. She saw his talent early on. On one of those occasions, she even bought a little drawing he had done at the Fleischer Art Memorial. As a twenty-year old, Peter went to one of the parties given by Barnes's alumni, and someone asked Violette, "If Dr. Barnes were alive now, whom would he buy?" Without missing a beat, she said, "He'd buy Peter Paone." "And that's the kind of person she was," said Paone, "she was wonderful."

How did she come to be the Violette de Mazia that we knew at the Barnes in the twentieth century, that wonderful woman whom Paone had met that day long ago? What were

Violette de Mazia's roots? What prompted her to leave her family in England to settle in the United States? How and where did she gain the experience that would mold her into a much esteemed and valued instructor? To know who she was and how as Director of Education of the Art Department at Barnes, she helped to develop a ground-breaking approach to the understanding and appreciation of art, we must travel back more than a hundred years, and many miles.

Cimetière du Montparnasse

The first step in the quest to understand how Violette de Mazia came to be the extraordinary woman who helped develop one of the most significant approaches to the understanding of art was to start at the very beginning with a visit her maternal ancestors' family tomb at the Cimetière du Montparnasse in Paris. Even with a schematic of the cemetery in hand, it was difficult to locate the Fraenkel monument.[2] It was nearly invisible among myriad old monuments and headstones. Most inscriptions were easy to read, but here and there were some that had become polished to a blank slate over time.

After a failed two-hour hunt using a deductive method, a slow but thorough inductive method became the only option. Searching row by row, headstone by headstone, it was finally discovered in the Jewish section of the cemetery. Here was the tomb of Violette's maternal grandfather, Moïse Fraenkel, born June 14, 1838, deceased January 20, 1904, and maternal grandmother Olga (also known as Elka), born March 21, 1835, and deceased December 14, 1912.[3]

Six other family members were interred there as well. One name especially caught the eye: Marius Fraenkel, who was Violette's great uncle. Etched in the stone next to his name is Chevalier de la Légion d'Honneur. Marius was a physician and a minister of the interior in charge of the police. Violette came from a distinguished family; and, as it turns out, she would become the second person in it to receive French knighthood.[4]

Rue Chaptal in Levallois-Perret

Stella Bertha Violette Mazia was born at six a.m. on the 30th of August in 1896, in her family's apartment at 49 rue Chaptal in Levallois-Perret, a town on the outskirts of Paris between Neuilly and Clichy. The Upper Seine rolls through the town historically known for two main industries: the Clément-Bayard motorcars (Citroen) and the Eiffel Company where the Statue of Liberty and the Eiffel Tower were built.[5] Israel (also known as Jules) Sonny Mazia, her father, a thirty-one-year-old accountant, was a native of Bielsk. Her mother, Feige Fraenkel Mazia, known as Fanny, and Violette's only sibling, her brother, Georges, who was born in Paris nearly three years prior, all lived with Sonny's parents, Aaron Mazia and his wife, Ghitel.[6] Before her marriage, Fanny lived with her parents, Moïse and Olga Fraenkel, in Neuilly-sur-Seine, a commune in the western suburbs of Paris. Fanny and her parents had immigrated to France from Kamenetz-Podolsk, Russia in the last quarter of the nineteenth century. The home that exists today at 49 rue Chaptal is not the same dwelling where Violette was born at the turn of the last century, for it has only two floors and an attic and could not possibly have hosted the nineteen families—a total of sixty-six people—who resided in the apartment house where Violette was born in 1896. The older building was either demolished or possibly destroyed during the German bombing raid of Paris in June of 1940. The history of the current house begins circa 1941.

Many residents who lived with the Mazias at 49 rue Chaptal in 1896 were simply classified as "employees." Violette's grandfather, at fifty, was already retired. Ghitel, her paternal grandmother, was a "ménagère" or housewife. It is hard to pin down her father's occupation. It varied greatly in records. On one he was listed as an engineer, on another he is the director de la maison franco-suisse; and yet on another he was listed merely as an "expert" without specifying what field. On his marriage record, he was a *comptable*, or accountant. He may have been all them or none. He may even have been in Secret Intelligence, as he seemed to be very well informed at a crucial time, as we shall see later.[7]

St. Gilles

The Mazia family soon left the environs of Paris to live in St. Gilles, Belgium, an autonomous, vibrantly developing commune south of Brussels.[8] The family members did not all relocate at the same time, and dates of their official registration are mixed. Violette's father and his parents were actually listed as residents of Brussels as early as 1893, living at Boulevard du Hainaut 51, before Violette was even born. Since Sonny was not present at the birth of his daughter in August of 1896, it is quite possible that he was in Belgium at the time. Violette's mother and brother, Georges, resettled on November 19, 1898. Violette reunited with her family in Belgium on January 31, 1899. Who actually chaperoned her is not known. Undoubtedly, it was a very close relative, perhaps a grandparent. Violette's family seemed to be following her paternal grandparents to Belgium. It was, in actuality, a return to that country, for it was there that her father and his parents lived when they first left Russia.

Sonny and Fanny may also have thought St. Gilles was an ideal place for their family to live. During this period, the Belgian economy was marked by rapid growth and expansion. St. Gilles, adjacent to Brussels, was a well-planned and developing town and was certainly an ideal choice for the young family. The town had four newspapers, reflective of a high level of literacy. The musically talented Mazias were definitely attracted by the town's ten musical societies, and its own école de musique (school of music).[9] Schools existed for every age from the jardin d'enfants [kindergarten] to the adult school.

This was a fully "modern" town with all the public services: water, gas, lighting, and an efficiently run electric trolley service for commuters—something we might take for granted today, but certainly not then. Violette lived here from the age of two and one-half years to eighteen in a rented home at rue de Constantinople 57 and remained at the same address until the family's departure for England the summer of 1914.[10] Sonny is listed from 1900 until 1914 in the Belgium Almanack, the address and occupational directory of its time, as I. Mazia, ingénieur (engineer).[11] Among their neighbors were a clerk, civil servant, coal merchant, tavern keeper, cap maker, and a host of shopkeepers; this was a neighborhood where Sonny Mazia and his family fit in comfortably.

In early September 1902, Violette began her attendance at "l'école communale," the local primary school in St. Gilles, which was conveniently located at the corner of the very block where the Mazia family lived.[12] The school had fourteen classrooms, a gymnasium, kitchen, sewing room, and a canteen. The school program, led by Madame Daems, consisted of three consecutive two-year courses of study. A student who began attendance at the age of six would have completed her classes by the age of twelve. At the time that Violette attended l'école communale, very few students completed the full program.[13] Violette was one of the few who did.

Isabelle Gatti de Gamond

After the completion of her coursework at l'école communale, Violette entered the Isabelle Gatti de Gamond School's *Cours Supérieur*, or upper school—the equivalent of high school—in the *Section Des Humanities*, a three-year course of study that included five languages—French, Flemish, English, German, and Italian; the history of concepts in literature; comparative literature of modern languages; bookkeeping; the elements of the natural sciences; practical handicrafts; vocal music; gymnastics and dance.[14]

Girls' secondary schooling was almost exclusively organized by Catholic nuns, prior to Gatti establishing her alternative school for girls. With its advanced approach to education, Gatti's school at rue du Marais 64, in the center of Brussels, attracted a number of gifted young girls. Less than two miles from her home in Saint Gilles, Violette could easily walk there in a half-hour or less. The electric tram, established in Brussels in 1894, was an alternative. With her gift for languages, her superb memory, and her athletic ability, Violette must have been a shining pupil. Along with eight other students in her class, she completed the course of study and received a *Certificat D'Études*.[15] A special award was granted to her and two other young ladies in her class at the

August 1914 graduation. Violette was given the certificate "in absentia," as she and her family had fled to England before that date, narrowly escaping the German invasion of Belgium at the onset of World War I.[16]

Fleeing to England

Sometime between late July and early August 1914, the Mazias left their home in Brussels and worked their way to England. No letters, or documents exist detailing the specifics of this exit from Belgium, so the route they took is unknown. The most direct course would have been the channel crossing from Antwerp. Several companies ran passenger service between Antwerp and cities in England. The Great Eastern Railway operated two ferries, the *SS Brussels* and the *SS Dresden*, built specifically for the Harwich–Antwerp service.[17] Since Violette and her family left dangerously close to the time of the August siege of Belgium, the most rapid and direct route could have made the difference between life and death, yet going by ferry also became increasingly dangerous, as German U-boats began to dominate the sea.

For this reason, Violette's family may not have taken the most direct and obvious route. It is said that Georges spent WWI in neutral Norway—to spare his life without a doubt—and during that time he mastered Norwegian, maintaining that knowledge in later years by listening to the Norwegian news on BBC radio every morning. Might the Mazias have traveled first to Norway and left their son Georges with a family there? There are no existing records to prove this, but if it were so, the Mazias might have remained there until Georges was reasonably acclimated. This would have given them sufficient time to make arrangements, solidify plans, and get the necessary travel documents for passage to and resettlement in England.

The Steamship Company operated a passenger service from West Norway to the United Kingdom during this time—specifically, the run from Bergen to Newcastle.[18] Though seemingly out of the way, the route to England via Norway may have been an extremely smart move because it was indirect and unique. It may have been the safest path to travel in the days immediately preceding the outbreak of war.

Whatever special intelligence or keen insight the family had, to make them decide to leave when they did, likely spared them a dire outcome. Had Violette and her family remained in Brussels, they would have faced certain starvation. If they tried to flee later, they would have been caught among hordes of people with the same intention. It could easily have ended tragically. About two months later, the inhabitants of Vivoorde, Wespelaer, Aerschot—eight, twenty-three, and twenty-miles, respectively, from Brussels—were attacked by German soldiers, and over two hundred unarmed innocent civilians slain in Aerschot alone.[19]

Boundary Road in St. John's Wood

*A*rriving in London at eighteen, during the beginning of WWI, it would have been practically impossible for Violette to continue her education.[20] Life was disrupted for nearly all—not just the thousands of recent émigrés. But Violette, gifted with an adaptability that helped her to thrive in a different country with a different language, set upon mastering the language of her new home at the Priory House School, north of the Thames river, on Alexandra Road in South Hampstead.[21] Years later, when she applied for an extension of her Visa to the United States, she would ask the Principal of the school, Jeanette Barnett, for a reference to send to the American Consul. Miss Barnett wrote that she had known Violette for many years, that not only had she "acquired English" there, but had become a teacher of French, geometry, and algebra in the school, preparing several girls for the Senior Oxford Local which they passed with honors. The coeducational school with sixty students in attendance was barely a skip from their first home on Boundary Road in England, and a short walk from their more spacious home on Fellows Road.[22] Soon after acquiring English, Violette decided to perfect her Italian, and by 1918 passed with distinction her viva voce and written examinations at the London Polytechnic (now known as the

University of Westminster).[23] Along the way, she also learned shorthand. With her keen memory learning the symbolic phonetic system developed by Sir Isaac Pitman might have seemed nearly effortless.[24] Violette used the system frequently in later years when she took notes at the Barnes, particularly when interviewing thousands of prospective students. With her knowledge of multiple languages and stenographic skill, she was eminently desirable as a secretary for companies that did business abroad. At that time, the Chamber of Commerce listed graduates of their Commercial Education department in their business catalogue with descriptions of their skills in language and stenography. Certainly Violette would have been listed, and eagerly hired. She would do her part to provide economic support for her family, recently exiled.

The Pitman's School in London was barely a two-block walk to the British Museum. It is easy to imagine Violette taking the opportunity to walk there after class to sketch, and study paintings and sculptures. She may have begun to merge her constantly improving linguistic and shorthand skills into a quick and efficient way of writing about the centuries of grand artwork she observed in the museum galleries. We should note another important influence. Her family was musically talented, and with their two grand pianos, harmonium, and violin, they often held musical soirees at their spacious home. Though Violette may not have been as talented as they were, she was sensitive to, and extremely knowledgeable about music.

The Love of Two Brothers

It was in London that Violette grew from a teenager into a young woman. Charming and brilliant, she inspired the strongest affection in others. Two admirers were brothers—students at the University of London in the first quarter of the twentieth century, who came from a well-to-do Sephardic Jewish family in Cairo. They would play a key role in the life of Violette. The younger brother, Elie Catz, declared his love first, and sent her a poem in French he had titled: *A une petite Violette douce comme l'aurore…fraîche comme la rosée du matin*, or "To a little Violette as sweet as the dawn…fresh as the morning dew." It reveals the depth of his passion. "If you read, Violette, the secrets of my soul, and if you knew my feelings for you, your darling little heart, your sweet heart of a woman, would perhaps think tenderly of me. If you knew how I would like to see you, Cherie, to tell you of my love for you, perhaps you would hear my poor bruised voice, pleading fearfully that you did not listen. If you knew, Viva, how I would wish you to tell me your dreams and your secrets, to bare your soul to me and give me your heart that you live always in eternal Happiness. My delicate little Violette, fresh as the dawn with beautiful azure blue eyes and long golden hair, this voice that begs you night and day, it is the voice of my heart, it is the voice of love."[25]

Elie signed it and added a note: "May you remember these verses in years to come, from Lily [Eli's nickname] who loved you so."

Later that year, Elie's older brother Joseph (Joe) became smitten with Violette; pursued her friendship and won her heart. Much to Joe's dismay, his younger brother continued to write Violette fifteen-page letters. Elie never stopped adoring his Viva, his Violette "so full of life." He even sent Joe a book for "Miss Violet" [sic] and asked her to "excuse him for his boldness but it was such a beautiful book he could not keep himself from making her aware of it." He would, in fact, send her dozens of treasured books throughout her lifetime.[26]

It was an instant attraction when Joe first met Violette in London, September of 1920. He realized immediately the beauty and complexity of her nature; knew that she was not easily read, a force to be reckoned with, and sometimes simply unknowable.[27]

Even several years later, aboard the *SS Mantua* as a new recruit in the Royal Air Force (RAF), Joe wrote: "I fell in love with you the first time I was in your presence. I barely knew you then, and even now perfect knowledge of your soul is a difficult problem I have barely begun to solve. You have always lived in a world apart, inviolate, access to which remains absolutely forbidden to passing strangers. But there is a blessed place where a hint of you may be divined. More expressive than words, your eyes, like faithful mirrors, reflect your inner turmoil. Tranquil lakes where your soul loves to gaze at itself. But their language is sometimes so obscure and incomprehensible! What haven't I suffered, even feared from the inscrutability of your expressions!"[28]

Violette was brilliantly, vividly, almost extravagantly vocal as a teacher, but reticent socially. It is what others say about her or to her, whether in memos, lengthy letters, and certainly in interviews that opens the door to knowing her. That is the case with the treasure trove of letters from her fiancé, Joe.[29] His communications certainly describe his devotion to her, as well as the personality and character of the man she was planning to marry, but they also tell us something about her. Joe and Violette seemed to have been opposites in character and disposition: Violette, the stable, quiet, extremely intelligent, highly skilled and scholarly individual; Joe, the adventurer, the committed and fearless soldier, dashing through life with boundless energy and devotion to special causes. He soared up to and through the clouds yet fought battles in all of life's arenas.

Though too young at sixteen, Joseph Catz joined the Zion Mule Corps by stowing away aboard the SS *Manitou*, appearing only when he was halfway to Gallipoli.[30] The details of Joseph's adventure were memorialized by the journalist Vladimir Jabotinsky.[31]

"In March 1915, at the camp, near Alexandria, Lieutenant-Colonel John Henry Patterson announced that Jewish volunteers would be recruited for the Zion Mule Corps.[32] Most of the recruits were refugees who were expelled by the Turks. The youth was admitted into the battalion when it was forming in Alexandria, but on the next day the relatives of the youth went to Patterson and produced certificates that proved that Josepf Katz [sic] was not a refugee and that his father was a well-known and respectable agronomist in Cairo and that the youth was merely sixteen years of age. Only boys who passed their eighteenth year were admitted into the army.

Young Joe was sent back from the camp to his house, and his entreaties were of no avail. A few days later the battalion sailed from Alexandria; after the boat had passed half the way from Alexander to Gallipoli, there appeared from the bottom of the ship a slim youth, who, with a sweet smile presented himself to [Joseph] Trumpeldor and Patterson. Surreptitiously boarding the ship in Alexandria, Joseph Catz served with the battalion throughout the Gallipoli Campaign."[33]

Though wounded twice, Joe remained in battle, playing a vital role at Gallipoli delivering water and urgently needed ammunition. Those in the trenches were less exposed to enemy fire than the mule drivers.

After Gallipoli, Joe was transferred to the Labor Corps and worked on the Ludd-Haifa Railway, then demobilized at Kantara Camp in Egypt. He worked as secretary to Vladimir (Ze'ev) Jabotinsky after WWI. From December of 1919 until Joe began flight training with the RAF, he was an instructor in Arabic and French for the Cairo Brigade. The education officer of the Brigade saw him as being "both zealous and energetic," and knew him to be interested in pursuing a commercial career.[34] But his goal seemed to be more complicated than that. He also planned to work in the Palestine Civil Service under Great Britain. The one thing he was sure of was that he planned to marry Violette de Mazia at the end of December in 1923, when his training as a fighter pilot was successfully completed.

In Alexandria, Joe was stationed at the No 4 Flying School outside of Cairo at Abu Sueir. Away from Violette from July to December of 1923, he began a long correspondence of hundreds of pages in a mixture of French and English that revealed the depth of his commitment and love, his romantic and poetic turn of phrase, but also the trials of this period. His letters started on the ship from Marseilles to Alexandria and continued through his flight training at Abu Sueir, Egypt, revealing much about his relationship with Violette as well as the relationship that Violette had at home with her family in London.

Absence Is to Love What Fire Is to the Wind

"l'absence est a l'amour ce qu'est au feu le vent, elle eteint le petit et ravive le grand."[35]

On the *SS Mantua* on the way to Alexandria, on July 29, 1923, Joe wrote to Violette that he felt so downhearted. "My heart seems to have stopped beating. My head aches, I feel I'm practically strangled to death and all I can do is to let my heart throb as it has continually been doing since God last allowed me to notice your divine little arm waving at me from the pier."[36] He had never felt this way before, his "head seemed so heavy and his nerves seemed to burst." His thoughts were always with her; and the farther the boat moved from shore, the more his thoughts of them together found harbor in his heart. No matter how far away he traveled, he knew there would be an intense connection between them...between his soul and hers.[37]

Joe found her presence at the pier empowering. "You know, all the time you kept your hand over your head, waving, I kept feeling so sure of myself, so brave, so happy, so invincible; and when I could no more see your arm above your head, étendu vers moi [extended toward me], all my assurance in myself drifted away from me and down went beautiful pride...." But then Violette would stretch her arm out toward him again, and once more he would feel "all conquering." Now in his mind, he could see her arm stretched all the time... "very plainly waving" and felt "triumphant and glorious...happy to have unearthed a divinity and took her unto me as my fiancée, the mother of all my thoughts, the sister of all my troubles, the friend of all my joys and the partner of all my heart and soul."[38] Joe left no emotion unexpressed. Violette meant everything to him. She was his goddess.

But it was not all perfection. Violette's father was not pleased with the match. And he must have shown this, for Joe certainly felt tormented by her father's mixed message: a seeming acceptance of him, then a resistance. Three months later, Joe wrote from the *SS Mantua* that "at times, he wished God never put him in her way, and others that He never gave him life." He even wished at one moment of supreme excitement that God would suppress forever all sensations and feelings of love in him.[39] Altercations and disputations they both had with her father occurred long and late into the night and made Joe feel utterly miserable for the pain it personally caused Violette.[40]

From the RAF base in Abu Sueir in Egypt, Joe continued the stream of letters to Violette. The first was an account of his daily routine: "Waking at 4:15 in the morning, flying by 5 a.m., continuing until 7:15, then breakfast until 8:40, daily, then prayer for 15 minutes. You see, out here, God is never lost sight of and it is a good thing too!" Classes started at 9 a.m.—three classes every day with a quarter-hour break after each course, which lasted one hour. At 12:45 work finished." His first thought of the day and the last before bedtime was always of Violette.

The weather was not at all extreme there, even an improvement over the greater heat in London when he was there just six weeks earlier. It wasn't a quiet spot with its "innumerable Avros constantly buzzing. The humming of an aeroplane stiffens your heart strangely…the continual buzzing of the machines' most powerful engines seem to push your heart right back and blend it with steel."[41]

Joe settled into a routine at the camp, and on the weekends he traveled hours by train to his family home on Maghrabi Street in Cairo. He counted the days until he would see Violette again, even visualizing the scenario on the way back from Egypt to Violette, the "ideal of his very soul and being." On the 28th day of December, he would leave Alexandria on the *SS Lloyd Triestino* at 1 p.m., and four and a half days later he would step foot at Liverpool Street Station in London: "[T]hen only shall I feel myself, my whole self again for… I departed from Tilbury Docks a skeleton, leaving behind the remainder of the attributes which make man the image of God in all meanings of the term…. So that the both of us might take pleasure in a heart and soul we must unite indissolubly for the rest our life here on earth and beyond…"[42] While he was in London, he was going to use every means to persuade the Air Council to permit him to continue his service at one of the training centers in England. He had little hope that he would be successful, but romantic Joe felt if the Air Marshall saw the depth of his love for Violette, he might approve. If he didn't, he would have to "wrap her up very warmly in his heart and bring her back with him to the Land of King Tut." In fact, he had already secured housing in Ismaëliah for them. "So be ready, darling fiancée of mine… for a thundering speedy wedding and a not less speedy departure for Egypt in the event I cannot succeed to remain in England for which I really have not more than one thousandth of a chance."[43]

But all along, Violette's father would switch back and forth, sometimes accepting that Violette and Joe would marry, and sometimes acting as though he never would. As Joe said, "I wonder what your father is thinking. Your letter received today states that your father has again dived into dead silence about our wedding…your father is playing a very cruel game on you by first applauding your efforts and then drifting into indifference."[44] It may have been that Violette kept her personal life to herself and did not tell her father all that passed between her and Joe. He hinted in his letters that her father had been "all the time trying to find out all what took place between the two of them." Joe assured her that despite this, they would marry in January 1924. And if her father did not accept their union, they would go to live in Egypt.[45] He signed his letter with the Italian version of his name—Beppo—and sent her "a million kisses."[46] He certainly meant it. But Violette's family remained in denial and tried everything to make her stay in the "family nest," silencing any discussion about marriage.[47] "How cruelly you are suffering," wrote Joe, "in you deepest emotions through your people at home so unwittingly choking all outward expression of your unbounded joy and happiness at the impending imminent realization of the supreme event for which both of us have been pining ever since September 1920."[48] All the "compensating pleasures" her family offered her were "only meant to sweeten a bitter drink"[49]

In two months and two days, Joe planned to meet Violette at Liverpool Street at 9 a.m. "I will embrace you if you come alone to meet me, but will embrace you all the same even if you are accompanied, tho' with eyes only!"[50]

That was the hypothetical scenario. There were letters coming and going between Violette and Joe, but it would be letters between their mothers that Joe thought would resolve any resistance to their union.

"My mother's letter [Clementine's] to your mother [Fanny] and both my letters addressed to you to Fellows Road constitute, I believe, the maximum required to make things clear and win over your father and your mother to us. You will admit that if all this fails, then it will be an utterly hopeless job to win over your father to our cause by peaceful means. But be convinced of one thing, that is, that whether he does side with us now or whether he does not, he is bound to come round sooner or later. He will, whatever you may think of his stubbornness. He will, for his own tranquility of conscience; for no human being has yet been known to keep up forever his amour-propre at the complete sacrifice of his love and duty towards his own and only daughter."[51]

With all his coaxing and enthusiasm, Joe's soaring highs were matched with the reverse. Though ten days prior Joe assured Violette that they would have a paradise together, he would crash back to earth and write Violette about "what she was letting herself into by marrying 'a Job.'" Escaping from his room to hide in an RAF hangar on the base that was closed to everyone at that extremely late hour, he wrote without interruption: "There is a vital point I still want to entertain seriously but have not done so far. It is a glaring fact: that although on one side we are readier to get married in less than two months, we have only built in the ideal atmosphere of love and romance. Although we are 'on holiday' together in almost all the areas of human sentiments and have triumphed gloriously in so much that we have obtained the proof we both possess the same 'outlook on life' even in the surplus of the most beautiful love, the more mobile and most ideal, however, we have done very little in the purely worldly phase which during our whole life will accompany our spiritual and loving union."[52]

Although Joe could give Violette everything that was necessary on a loving and spiritual level, he could not compete with the material benefits Violette had by living with her family. Joe knew from one of her recent letters that her mother was fitting up a new private *cabinet de toilette* for her, and her father was doing all he could to make her feel as comfortable as possible at Fellows Road. In Joe's opinion this was done in order to make her fully realize what she might lose if she abandoned her family's home to marry him and to appreciate to the fullest extent what she would be missing in her new home in Abu Sueir.[53]

"No such comfort can be found in an Air Force officer's home," he wrote. "I could not attempt to think what casing should harbour such a gorgeous jewel as you…I have enough love to last for eternity…but fortune…never, never, can be our share. I never aspired to be rich, but never as today have I have so wanted to become for you…."

"You lost material benefits by coming to me. This is the sad reality. My entire love for you is enough to last for eternity, whatever happens, under whatever sky in whatever age; but fortune, I believe strongly, never, never, can be our share. I never aspired to be rich, but never as today have I have so wanted to become for you…."

"But what is called the greatest love would not resist the adversities of nature, that a little girl who has never lacked material comforts cannot be completely happy with a husband with very little money…."

"It is indispensable for two reasonable beings, before they seal their lives together forever, to thoroughly study all contingencies of their married life in every possible aspect. For myself I have done so most thoroughly and the verdict is that: I love you. I want you. I'll be happy, the happiest of all men, only with you as my moral and legal wife."

"...do the same, scrutinize every corner of your heart and of your brain, and tell me in all its sweetness as well as its bitterest bitterness all that finds room in you. Bear also well in mind that it may mean you having to abandon all your relatives and relations for good if they persist in condemning our wedding until it has been accomplished, for to grant us forgiveness after our wedding when they would have done everything in the world to wreck it would be very extremely serious; and I, for one, shall not accept it, at least as far as it concerns me personally."

It is likely that Violette did "scrutinize every corner of her heart," and that Joe was content with her response. It was not Violette who would put a damper on their love, but her father. He was the embodiment of silence. It was possible Sonny de Mazia did not want his Violette to be wrested away from them to faraway Egypt and, in particular, married to a fighter plane aviator who planned to migrate to Palestine after the marriage. Joe had, after all, spent several years as the special assistant to Jabotinsky, who was instrumental in the building of a Jewish self-defense organization in Palestine. "The silence of your dad torments me more than I like to admit," he wrote to Violette. He deduced that her parents might be more agreeable to their marriage if he were posted in England; and, as previously noted, he was already searching for a way to be posted for at least one of his terms at the RAF station in Uxbridge, England.[54] Seventeen miles from Fellows Road was a hop away compared to the more than 3000 miles between Cairo and London.

Violette's father was not the only challenge Joe faced. Attaining a high level of proficiency on the Avro so that he would be stationed in England was also foremost in his mind. He felt the need for more flight experience and did not yet even feel equipped to do a solo flight. Sheer luck had gotten him this far, but he could not rely merely on fate or chance in something so potentially dangerous: "… the day I had to go solo, three weeks ago, the planes smashed, then it was the Fog! Yes, the fog here in Egypt, (at 6 am of course) and after lunch (9:30 am) the atmosphere is too bumpy and thus unfit for instruction; and now it is I who would wish to delay, delay, my solo until the last minute, so as not to let myself miss the thousandth chance to save you the grief of your marriage without the approval of your father, perhaps in a successful transfer to Uxbridge."[55]

Joe's safety during flight training was a concern. There were fifty-three fatal crashes in the RAF from January to December 15, 1923.[56] Violette, her family and Joe's family must have been aware of the fatalities, if not from news reports or by word of mouth, at least instinctively. Joe, aware of the risk, wrote to his older sister Rose that he regretted nothing.[57]

"Why torment yourself? If it must happen it is going to be, if something is going to happen it will as easily on terra firma as in the air. I am not a fatalist in anything concerning the progress of nature and the efforts to deploy or to fail to achieve a goal in life; but as for Life itself, I am not of the opinion that human beings can make the least bit of difference. To live or to die is in God's hands alone. That's why I do not torment myself on this subject. I have elected to enter aviation knowingly, in full knowledge of the facts. I regret nothing. I can foresee in my success a great good that one day will follow me to the land of Israel, and that is enough to pay me back infinitely for being in the Air Force. Even the eventuality that I'll never be able to serve in my homeland and to die before even having the consolation that Moses had before dying contemplating the land of Israel from the sky in my Avro, like Moses on the mountain, despite being aware of this possibility, I do not have any hesitation to say that I would die happy even in the my training period, in order to serve one day in Palestine."[58]

The flying conditions worsened at this time. The morning fog kept Joe from flying before 9 a.m. for two weeks; and the morning after 9 a.m. was not a propitious time for new solo flyers because air pockets formed after that hour, and the airplanes could fall many yards suddenly and unpredictably. Only expert pilots could venture forth in these tricky conditions. Joe's plane was also in repair for quite a while; it wouldn't be until Thursday or Friday, November 22nd or 23rd, that he could go solo in the airplane before 6 a.m.; that is, if the fog held off. He was exuberant about it. "The time when I will go alone in the air that is when the 'fun' will begin. I will continue to do it everyday from 6 to 8:30 and 9:45 to 11:15. I flew yesterday for a half hour accompanied by an instructor but I did all the maneuvering by myself and at the same time executed a Spin [downward spiral] with the engine off, imitating an accidental fall of 3000 feet and coming out of the spin, re-stabilizing the plane. I 'aced' it. This 'Spin' is one of the most dangerous aerial acrobatics, but I don't find it any scarier than the simplest somersault and the instructor told me that I did it to perfection."[59]

Joe considered Violette to be his good-luck charm, his talisman. "I am sure that it is thanks to your having slept 'with a closed fist' and thus held your thumbs in the hollow of your hands on the dates I was supposed to go solo, it is thanks to that that I did not go up solo, which obviously means some crash would have ensured had I done so."[60] Accidents did happen. Just two days after he wrote the above to Violette, Joe was being tested for his solo, going into a beautiful spin, and coming out of it a second before a deadly crash. "I took off with terrific speed and was a hair from bumping against the steel hangar in front. Suddenly the engine failed, and there I was spinning towards infinity! In short I very nearly killed myself, the examiner, and pulverized the machine...." The examiner reported him to the authorities as being too sure of himself and with a temperament extremely "dashing, impetuous and reckless and most unsafe to venture with!" Joe actually blamed the incident on the instructor for bawling him out in the air, "If any of them tells me off, I do become reckless!"[61] He was very confident that if they let him go solo, he could completely satisfy his instructors.

Joe's family was obviously concerned. At the least, they were alerted by the inauspicious weather pattern for flying; and, though daily reports of casualties at the RAF base might have been censored, informal gossip about the multitude of flight fatalities must have existed. And there were many accidents at RAF bases. From November 12, 1918, to December 14, 1923, there were 649 reported fatalities. Just the day before his "tribulations in the air," Joe received Rose's letter reflecting the family's fears about what might happen. And something did happen on that day! Even though Joe was aware of the dangers of flying the Avro, he thought the letter showed an extraordinary prescience.[62]

"It is so heartbreaking that four months of effort are annihilated by a half hour of impetuosity in the air," Joe wrote to Violette. "My commander said this to me: 'Look here Catz, you mustn't think there is the slightest disgrace in not possessing the right temperament to fly.'" His commander saved even harsher criticism for others. The "Latin races" were "far too excitable to fly at all." The French were "rotten aviators; most courageous but most hog headed and unreliable! Turks could never fly. I haven't known a single Turk aviator! So don't be distressed; some of the brainiest and cleverest men I knew could not take the machine off the ground after months of training; it's just a question of temperament."[63]

But Joe had his own special hero to emulate. He had read the poem "Bruce and the Spider," by Bernard Barton, when he was nine, and since that day he always did his utmost to live up to it. He would be patient, have courage, and persevere. "Should I shake the foundations of the Air Ministry at Kingsway to the very core of its foundation, so they will grant me a solo flight before considering me beaten." "Don't say a word of this to any one, darling. This is strictly between me and you and that's the way it must remain."[64]

The next day, November 16th, Joe wrote that he had "not killed anybody in the Air today," nor had he injured himself. In fact, he did "exceedingly well" and was going up again the following Monday. One sign of stress on his part, though, was a little headache he admitted to having as he bid Violette, the "little darling of his heart" a sweet good night and signed "love Beppo" to one more adoring letter.[65]

The following week, Monday the 19th, Joe wrote, "Here I am, still alive after his morning's flip." Even with this event, he felt "steady again and as master of [his] controls as ever." He had gone home to Cairo during the weekend to quell his mother's anxieties about him; and, he thought, seeing him "in flesh and blood did tranquilize her immensely." He was sure that once he went "solo successfully" she would "feel quite all right." Weather permitting it would be the next day; but if it were like this day without wind, it wouldn't happen. No wind was bad for flying.[66]

The conditions did not change the next day, but Joe received a letter from Violette that brought him "immense happiness." Her parents had finally accepted their forthcoming marriage. "Thanks to you my darling, for, had it been left to me entirely to pull this through, I should long ago have lost patience and carried you off never to reset our eyes on 63 Fellows Road and its precious inhabitants. You have indeed revolutionized my whole being; you have even changed my nature for never on earth should I have thought anything in this world could thus succeed to make me wait three years for what I had decided to do after the first five minutes I spent with you. But was it not worth it! See it was, and, as you know, had I had to wait three times as much and more, I would wait, for, was it the reaffirmation of the loftiest idea of my heart, my soul and every particle of my body! The challenge was great, dazzling. I came and saw and waited. Now I won you wholly with your perfect happiness unimpaired and not in the least crippled thro' wounds for the want of love." [67] No one could accuse Joe of lack of exuberance.

Rose, Joe's sister, would write to Violette about the dressing requirements in "Pharoah Land"—as he expressed it—but personally Joe felt that one wore the same things as in England, especially in winter. Summers were less warm in Egypt, at least compared to the ones he spent in London. "Don't, don't alter any of your fancies in dresses or tastes in shades; whatever you'll wear here will become the fashion after you have worn it once, for you wear things so well that really it strikes the world as the ideal."[68]

Joe also told Violette in the same letter that he had saved sufficient funds for both of their travel fares back to Egypt. He would be the proud possessor of about £150 on his "alighting in London" and that would leave a margin of £50 or so for "oddments." They would have about £40 a month to live on when they returned to Egypt. "You will see, cherie, we will manage." Joe had already made arrangements for them to live in Ismailia for the six months until the end of his flight training. He had committed to a small apartment and garden with pension from a Madame Guillet, who would take care of everything—meals, laundry, cleaning. Violette, Joe promised, would "not have the hassle of settling in."[69]

Pressure was building as final exams approached, and Joe apologized to Violette for not writing to her as much as he would like since he had to study from morning to night. Even so, he dedicated one particular evening to her, and poetically added: "as indeed are all the minutes of my life"—to writing to her "right into the deepest depth of the night until my eye lids begin to droop and continue to do so till I can no more see and the ink dries in my pen...."[70]

In three weeks, Joe was scheduled to wend his way back to Violette—by train from Abu Sueir to Port Said, across the sea to Marseilles on the P & O Kalyan or China.... "Thence by rail towards the very best of myself."[71] Meanwhile, he sent by certified mail his birth certificate and naturalization papers in case she needed them for immediate preparations. He visualized staying barely a week in London before they would head back to North Africa. There was no doubt in his mind that military leave would be granted as he had already spent two summers at the base. A report "full of praise" had just been sent to the chiefs of staff saying he was "the Steady and Reliable pilot of the place!" even after the exploit in which he nearly flew an Avro into the ground with him and his instructor in it! "But," he said, "of course, that only happened once, and was meant to put the 'wind up' a fellow who indulged in bullying. I knew all the time I'd get away with it in time."[72] He promised Violette he would not "try such stunts in future, despite any provocation." In his letter to Violette on November 23rd, Joe would boast of "three wonderful solos."[73]

Yet, the "steady and reliable pilot of the place" had to admit to Violette on the very next day "I've had a crash! [The underlining here was Joe's emphasis.] This morning. The first one! The 4th of December. Kind of 'baptism by fire' … Yet don't worry, don't. It's alllll [sic] right. Nothing broken, I mean, nothing of me. No bones, not even a contusion." Around the time of his letter—before and after—Joe sent Violette several comic sketches illustrating his flight events. One, entitled "First trip—*D'apres Dick la farceur*," [First trip—Following Dick the Trickster], Joe said would give her a "rough idea of what happened. Being somewhat of an acrobat I jumped off my Savoy Avro in good time." In reality, there was damage to the plane —a bent axle, a broken compression structure, one wheel blown away, but jokester Joe preferred the comic version. There being, according to his account, a "general reproach from the members of the Brighter Tarmac Society for having performed in the desert, robbing them of the most exalting entertainment of the Avro 3547's quack pilot."[74]

Ironically, at least according to Joe, his flight instructors were "DELIGHTED (sic) about the whole matter!!!—They said I put up an excellent show, because I positively took up the machine in the air as soon as another strut, axle, and wheel had been fixed to it and not waiting for instructions, flew off and executed further aerobatics and made three extra fine landings! So all's for the best," he wrote to his darling Vio.[75]

Violette sent letters to Joe on November 22nd, 23rd, and 24th (known only because Joe mentioned it in this letter to her, as they no longer seem to exist) assuring him that at this juncture, everyone "rallied completely" to their union including, most importantly, her father. "It is indeed a most soothing feeling…of having the whole world happy at our coming future wedding. I was still anxious about your father's real sentiments regarding me. I still believed he might have only agreed to the wedding as a last resort, to save you unnecessary renewed sufferings but what you tell me about his remarks regarding my letters …make me feel that perhaps he really does like me after all and is happy that I am becoming his second son."[76]

Joe had also recently received a long letter from Colonel Bentwich, the attorney general in Palestine, in response to a letter he had written to the colonel describing his first solo flight; and though Joe had disappointing news from a fellow officer in Abu Sueir about Jews serving in Palestine, he held the strong conviction that his duty lay in going no matter what, and that he would do so despite the naysayers.[77] To serve as a soldier in Palestine seemed to have been Joe's immediate if not ultimate career goal.

Obviously Violette was upset about the crash on December 4th, but Joe felt she should feel the opposite. "My 'do' of the 4th should rather cheer you up than the contrary for to have a crash and get away without a scratch and only damage the machine in such a way as to have her on 'her wings' again within an hour, is pretty good."[78] His instructor and commanding officer were actually optimistic about it. A crash "does a tremendous amount of good to an 'aspiring' pilot." In their mind, it calmed the pilot down. Joe did not agree with their logic but understood their reason for thinking it.[79]

Joe had a break of ten minutes between courses when he wrote to Violette about his travel plans to England two weeks hence. The plans were vaguely described, for though he knew he would be traveling by a P & O Steamer at Port Said, which steamer it would be he did not know for sure. He would be arriving at a station in London, but he did not know which one exactly. He would telegram to let her know "in good time."[80]

Even though Joe was "drowning" in his studies for the Gurney Engines and Law Examinations, he would find the time to walk to his "pigeon hole in the letter rack at the stroke of noon" to check for mail. "Not a word for Beppo," he wrote Violette. For five days during this time, he was also officer of the Watch, and had to keep a sharp look out for any aircraft from 6 a.m. to 6 a.m. — twenty-four hours around the clock studying and on watch without sleep. At this time, there was also an engagement party for his brother Elie, who had appealed to his older brother to travel to Cairo to celebrate with him. Joe left at 8 p.m. on Saturday night and reached home the next day at 10:15 a.m. It was a grand soiree, and he celebrated until 4 a.m. with the "third batch of guests." There were so many guests that there were three separate parties back to back with Perrier champagne, and "dancing around Vio's photos like fanatics around Buddha."[81]

Days without sleep had taken its toll. The next day Joe wrote to Violette, "I have come down from the heavens. I spent two and a half hours SOLO [sic] at camp, everything was topsy-turvy; search parties went to look for me all over the neighborhood, they thought I was lost, drowned, ablaze." He was expected to land after 40 minutes, but got "lost in the clouds," and as he described it, "bounced around with delight." He spent 2 ½ hours performing all kinds of maneuvers "using just the left hand."[82] Though Joe joked about it, we do not know the officers' reaction, and we can only imagine Violette's shock.

Several days later, Joe was in the midst of examinations when he wrote to Violette: "It was a nightmare," but he was happy to say his "solos" during an officer cadet exhibition went well. He was already transitioning from cadet to husband-to-be, when he asked Violette if she wanted him to marry in full dress. He had read in the *Daily Mirror* that their flight instructor married that way. "We'll do it if you like."[83]

"I shall go to Cairo today, for the final arrangements about my departure. See that you are completely ready in every way to get married by the 1st of January. It would be a lovely date for a wedding. It'll also coincide with somebody's birthday [Joe's!]. Oh, by the way I only got 31 days leave instead of 34 I first thought I would get. That's why my leave expires on the 23rd of January but even then, I may have to be back in Cairo by the 15th of January to pass exams in Arabic. This is important as it registers me as candidate on the staff. It may be I won't be able to sit in London, you see. Goodbye darling. I love you lots & lots & lots."[84]

This was Joe's last letter to Violette.

On December 17, at 3:51 in the afternoon, Joe became the very last of the 44 flight fatalities of the RAF in 1923. The official summary of the event in December was exceedingly brief. "During the month a fatal accident occurred to P/O.

[pilot officer] J. Catz who was killed in an Avro by spinning into the ground behind the village."[85] "Cause obscure" was noted on his Royal Air Force Casualty Card. The Court of Inquiry determined that though Joe did well "passing successfully through flight school," when he was actually "in the air," he seemed "unaware of the flying regulations regarding stunting below 2000 feet." In a puzzling message, they said "no responsibility rests on any individual," yet they blamed Joe's "foreign origin and excitable nature." He, in their opinion, "was not in reality a suitable type of Officer to select for training as a British officer."[86]

Was this "opinion" a hint about what Joe really wanted to talk about with Violette months back when he thought he might just leave Abu Sueir and the RAF but wanted to make sure he was accurate in his assessment? Did he suspect bigotry, a systemic prejudice?

The RAF described him as lacking the discipline of a British soldier, and it seemed he was a wanderer, literally and figuratively "lost in the clouds," but considering his intelligence, fearlessness, and bravery in the actual arena of war, it is hard to believe that mechanical failure of his Avro 1772 did not even seem to be seriously considered, though the nature and cause of the accident was deemed "obscure."

On the other hand, might Joe have deliberately gotten "lost in the clouds" on a suggestion, or even an order from Jabotinsky, to survey the terrain of the base and the area around it? Jabotinsky, a believer in self-defense, was soon to become the commander of the Irgun, a Zionist paramilitary organization in Palestine. Joe must also have personally known the Zionist activist and war hero Josef Trumpeldor, for the military hero was a cofounder of the Zion Mule Corps with Jabotinsky. Trumpeldor had also been the commander of the

Jewish defenders of Tel Hai in 1920. Did British Military Intelligence and/or Egyptian Intelligence conjecture this as well and consider Joe a potentially serious threat? After all, he was an ardent Zionist learning to fly a plane. It is possible that he was targeted, and his death not a mere accident, but the truth would be buried deep in the desert sand of Abu Sueir, and the restricted records of the RAF.

For their part, the Catz family considered Joe heroic, honorable, talented and worthy of a funeral befitting a military man of the highest caliber. After all, he had served in multiple arenas—Gallipoli, Mesopotamia, and Palestine— and was the first Jewish officer to enter Jaffa after the British occupation.[87] "Most impressive ceremony," wrote a reporter attending Joe's funeral in Cairo.[88] Six RAF officers escorted the caisson that was heavily and extravagantly festooned with exotic flowers. The funeral cortege passed through Opera Square in Cairo, in a procession through the city on the way to the Jewish cemetery.

Written memorials for Joe likened him to a chevalier, a knight—a Jewish knight.[89] "At an age where others are prone to childish games and abandon themselves to carefree indifference, he manifested the will to serve. Overcoming an alarmed opposition, he left his paternal home of his own free will; though his parents tried in vain to restrain him with their tender bonds, he joined the ranks of the British army to liberate the ancestral land from the Turkish yoke. In a moment, he had exchanged the costume of a young boy for a khaki uniform. To accomplish something great was the focus of his tireless activity. Certainly it was not for vainglory; modest, he felt it repugnant to boast falsely of bravery." But he wanted to "remind us of the genius, courage and heroism of the ancient Maccabees [who] embodied the highest sensibilities of the Jewish race under fire. And his soul exalted at the thought that he was one of the first Jewish soldiers after twenty centuries."[90] *Per ardua ad astra,* Joe wrote to Violette on the back of one of the handsome photos of him he sent her the summer of 1923—

"Through adversity to the stars." Joe reached for the stars, soared high above the earth, and met adversity head on.

Crossing the Sea

What anger Violette may have felt toward her parents—perhaps more specifically her father—for their resistance to her marriage to Joe Catz, we will never know, for nothing written has survived to describe it. Neither will we know what regret she had for her equivocation and doubt during the three years of Joe's courtship. But as the months of mourning passed, Violette began to plan her first transatlantic voyage to the United States. She was already in possession of a passport from travels to Belgium with her father in 1922, its photo showing Violette in a dark felt cloche-style hat, tweed coat trimmed with fur, wavy bobbed hair, and a somber yet calm look, with large eyes that seem to reflect a profound inner and outer vision. It is a searching look, as though she were studying us, the viewers. Here is not a Mona Lisa smile of contentment, but one that seems a blend of resolve and vulnerability, depth of character, strength with sensitivity and softness.

Violette's first crossing of the Atlantic was to Philadelphia to visit her cousins, the Bayuks on North Broad Street.[91] Samuel Bayuk, a millionaire cigar manufacturer by the 1920s, had encouraged her to visit the United States and wrote a reference for her to submit to the United States Consulate in London so that she could obtain a travel visa for her lengthy stay. Bayuk also paid for her passage on board the SS *Aquitania* departing from Southampton, England on May 17, 1924, five months to the day after Joe Catz was killed. Violette's original plan was to visit the Bayuks for three to five months, but she remained with them for six. To rest and recuperate was the principal reason for the trip; but travel, too, was primary, and this she did for a great part of this first visit to the States: to visit, and experience schools in Pennsylvania, and Ohio. Was she, in fact, already contemplating a teaching career in the United States? Her passport describes her as 5 feet 5 inches tall, with fair hair, fair complexion, and blue eyes. She lists her last address in the United Kingdom as "in transit," with the intention of becoming a permanent citizen of the United States. Mentally, she had already begun to break away from her family in London, and was planning the rest of her life.[92]

It is during this time that the Bayuks connected Violette with their well-to-do friends, the Silvermans—owners of a department store designed by Paul Philippe Cret at the southwest corner of Sixth and South Street—who wanted their daughter, Rosalie, to learn French. Rosalie, a centenarian at the writing of this book, explained how they came to meet. "Mrs. Bayuk and my mother were good friends. And when Violette arrived here, she needed some money. Mrs. Bayuk asked her friends, '"Does anybody want a tutor?' My mother said, 'Sure; I have a nine-year-old girl, and it would be wonderful if Violette would come to our house.'" That's how I knew her, through the Bayuks. Once a week, she would come to the house. I adored her. I started to learn French. That summer we were going to be in France. My mother knew that Violette was going to be in Paris when we were, and she arranged for us to meet. I knew Violette was going to meet us at our hotel. When I went down in the elevator, I was so excited that I was going to see Violette. When I got off the elevator, I jumped on her, and I almost knocked her down I was so happy to see her. We saw her a few times that summer. Violette tutored me French for two years. My connection was long-term. I never lost track of her, and we always knew where Violette was and what was going on. That's how I eventually went to the Barnes and took the courses with her."[93]

When Violette first arrived in Philadelphia to stay with the Bayuks, there were five children and an orphaned niece and nephew in their household, ranging in age from seven to twenty-three. The family certainly knew a thing or two about local schools, and Violette would certainly have asked for advice if not guidance. They may have suggested Miss Sayward's School and the Bryant Teachers Agency to find out if there were positions available. We know that Nelle E. Mullen, Dr. Albert C. Barnes's employee, inquired of the agency for a teacher of French in September of 1925; and she was given Violette's name.[94]

A talented teacher, Violette was soon hired to teach advanced mathematics and French in a school similar to that of Jeanette Barnett's Priory House School in London, preparing young ladies for their college and entry examinations. Miss Sayward's School on Drexel Road was in a newly developing upper-middle-class community in Overbrook, a suburb of Philadelphia. Both schools had women teachers, a governess, a cook, and servants; and all the faculty and domestics were single. A handful of the teachers and students were boarders, but by far most of students were daytime attendees.

That month, Bryant Teacher's Agency connected Violette with the Barnes Foundation to tutor French to three ladies twice a week for three hours.[95] At the same time, she was invited to attend the lectures given there by a young professor, Thomas Munro, a Dewey-influenced PhD who was then a visiting professor of Modern Art at the University of Pennsylvania.[96] A brilliant student, Violette quickly succeeded in synthesizing the Barnes philosophy with a Dewey-style experiential teaching method, and Barnes realized it.

Violette de Mazia's earliest letters to Albert Coombs Barnes were in French. One of these, from London in July of 1926, shows that she was establishing a working relationship with Barnes and seemed comfortable communicating with him. In these initial letters, Violette saw Philadelphia as her new home and the Barnes Foundation as her new haven.[97] Addressing him as Doctor, she advised him that she had: "applied for the 'quota' and the American Consul in London has asked for, among other documents, a letter from a person in authority or of good standing (an American citizen, but not a relative) who knows me well and can establish my character. I hope you will agree to the above-mentioned qualification and you will have the great kindness to send me such a letter to be delivered to the Consul—which would help me to cross the Rubicon." As to the purpose of her journey, she declared that it was to "study and teach." Violette was already assisting Barnes as a researcher. She had just visited the opening exhibition of the Modern Foreign Gallery at the Tate in London and sent Barnes the catalog of the exhibition. She wrote: "I found *Les Parapluies* of Renoir. They also have a portrait of a woman, with an all-bluish effect, very beautiful Daumiers, Manets, Degas. In Seurat's *la Baignade*, I did not find pointillism as I imagined it. All together it was significant enough, but a meager showing of Cézanne. Still, this vision has refreshed my memories."[98]

In all likelihood, one of her first tasks was mastering the reading list "A First Requisite in Art Education" compiled by Mary Mullen (a long-time employee of Barnes, and one of the original five trustees of the Foundation) making her way through works by Dewey, Ellis, McDougall, Santayana, Singer, Trotter, Barnes' *The Art in Painting*, Buermeyer's *The Aesthetic Experience*, and Mullen's *An Approach to Art*.[99] Mary Mullen's book was probably the first she tackled and perhaps it became her bible. It was written with an erudition and simplicity that made it the perfect primer for the Barnesian approach, a must for the diligent and studious neophyte.[100]

Mullen, via the philosophy of Schopenhauer, explained how to approach a painting: It was with silence. The philosopher "long ago pointed out that a picture should be looked at as a royal personage is approached, in silence, until the moment it pleases to speak to you, for, if you speak first, you expose yourself to hear nothing but the sound of your own voice."[101]

It is easy to imagine Violette carrying a copy of Mullen's primer by her side, day-by-day building a philosophical, aesthetic, and theoretical map to follow—not imitate. Violette skillfully brought this together with her gifts of superior analysis, eidetic memory, creative use of metaphors and analogies, and it would serve her well as she taught others. The Barnesian approach was a new way of looking, talking, and writing about art—akin to an artist's reaction to what she sees and experiences…a kind of personal enlightenment.

Violette's writings were based on first-hand experience. It is during her first decade in Philadelphia that Violette traveled regularly to Europe for the spring and summer months, usually arriving in France in May and departing for the States in August or September.[102] These were months devoted to extensive and intensive art research in European museums and churches for the Barnes Foundation. Ensconced in them daily, Violette took notes of what she saw, and they were passed on to Dr. Barnes, who was specific about what he wanted the Girls (Violette and Mary Mullen) to look for on these summer art excursions. It would be a mixed message. In Dr. Barnes' letter to them on the SS *Berengaria* the summer of 1927, he asked them to "use their own heads and eyes" on examining the Cologne pictures," but he also wanted them to find evidence to support his belief that the "early Germans were superior to the Flemings, Weyden and Gerard David, who [were] much more worshipped than these early comparatively unknown Cologne painters." Barnes felt the Cologne paintings were extremely important: "I don't think you can afford to miss them; they throw a light on the whole tradition of painting."[103]

Violette researched for the books she co-authored with Barnes' during that first decade, traveling by ship from New York to Southampton, or Plymouth, England in the spring of each year, and returning to the United States toward the end of August from Southampton, or from the northern ports of France; such as Le Havre or Cherbourg.

Barnes valued Violette's notes on paintings, and thought well enough of them to share them with others; in one case, with the philosopher-educator John Dewey. In March of 1931, when Violette had been with Dr. Barnes for a half-dozen years, and two years before they co-published *The Art of Henri Matisse*, the doctor sent Dewey the following note: "Your Tuesday lecture is on 'rhythm and balance as form'—

that's why I'm sending you a photograph of Matisse's big *Joie de Vivre* (*The Joy of Life*), together with Miss de Mazia's notes of two or three years ago upon which she based a talk to her class in front of the picture. If the notes are not too cryptic [her early notes have sections in Pitman shorthand that are fairly difficult to translate], with the photograph, [they] may enable you to give your presentation an objective turn."[104]

When the Matisse book was published, the artist sent Violette a thank you letter from his home at Place Charles Felix in Nice, France. He apologized that he could not find a translator to write a letter that would reflect the immense gratitude he felt for the enormous amount of work she and Dr. Barnes went through to write about his work. "This is a veritable opus. It saddens me today that I cannot sufficiently express to you how excellent its presentation is. I hope soon to have the pleasure of repeating my compliments in a more precise way at the home of mademoiselle."[105]

The Matisse book was the second one she co-wrote with Dr. Barnes. *The French Primitives* preceded it by two years. *The Art of Renoir* and *The Art of Cezanne* would follow them. Four books were published in fourteen years, all of them followed de Mazia's seminal essay on Stravinsky and Matisse published in *Art and Education* in 1929.

Early on, it also became apparent to the Mullen sisters, Mary and Nelle, just how much Violette's companionship meant. Mary wrote to Violette in early September of 1926, on her way back to the States after a summer's journey through the galleries of Europe. "First of all, I must tell you that we miss you very, very much, since we came away and left you all alone in Paris. When we first talked about our trip to Europe, we all (everybody at the office) agreed that it would be very profitable for each one of us, if you could come with Nelle and me to see the pictures, but we underestimated its joy and pleasure to be derived from your companionship that we shall always remember as something over and above its profit secured from studying the pictures together. We talk about you every day and wish that you could have come with us."[106]

A serious researcher, Violette would hop from painting to painting, fresco to fresco during the annual summer scholarly haunts of churches, galleries, and museums in Europe. From Florence during the summer of 1927, Violette wrote an account of one leg of their art pilgrimage. Leaving Michelangelo "to land at the feet of Giotto," they stayed three nights next door to Giotto's home at the Subasio Hotel, "in Assisi's other-worldliness," then the following night in Perugia. "We have just started on our way to Arezzo & will reach Florence by eight o'clock, to-night. This is the crude narrative of our staccato trip from Rome to Florence but the setting & background are the real substance of it. Seeing the pictures in their own native land plays a magical trick upon our imaginations & eyes. We can get the spirit of the traditions—in Dame Nature's terms—from wonderful landscape & scenery. Between Rome & Assisi, we enjoyed quite a few Giorgiones: the flow of the hills, of the Earth, the glow of the sun thru' half opaque clouds, then a foretaste of Giotto in his little cauliflower trees and angular little impossible cities behind a wall on the hills, all bathed in light & powdered lapis lazuli." Violette was sure that the Giottos she was revisiting were definitely better than they had ever been. Were they improving, or was she improving? The difference might have been from her experiences in Padua. Or was it the sequence that made the difference? Whatever it was, her pleasure was increased. They seemed nicer than her memory of them from the previous year. As if "the effect of somebody's closed hand being opened suddenly close to & in front of my eyes—sort of an electric current!" On the road between Perugia and Arezza, she felt as if she were travelling in the very middle of Perugino's space: "little strips of clouds overhead on which he perched his actors, but instead of the latter, we have the witches dancing in the foreground and some little Van-Gogh-y trees that bring us up to modern times." In jest, she added that she and Jeannette Portenar "had all the best intentions of packing up one of the frescoes in our bag, but we could not possibly decide on which one." They stayed at the Berchielli Hotel along the embankment of the Arno, a two-minute walk to the Ponte Vecchio, the bridge with the little shops, and near the galleries. When they arrived, it was dark and late and they couldn't see much of the town; nevertheless they loved Florence. "Leonardo at this moment would paint us both with turned up corners of the lips!"[107]

A month before Florence, Violette visited the Mauritzhaus at The Hague in Holland to study its paintings.[108] There were two Vermeer paintings, *Girl with Turban* and *View of Delft*, that she studied. The former with its sharp contrast of a light figure against dark background was a "trick" in her opinion; using the "dramatic effect of the light figure against a dark background rather than any plastic achievement.... The background was uniform, not a fine realization of distance. Color in dress brittle, no profundity, no feeling for essential qualities of stuffs." Familiar with Bernard Bosanquet's *Three Lectures on Aesthetics*—from the Barnes' Foundation list of required reading—and its concept of *étouffer* (stuffs or substance), she remarked that the quality of Vermeer's painted fabric lacked real substance.[109] Violette had objections as well to the blue band around the head and the ivory streamer. The painting of the textures in the turban and streamer were reminiscent of Ingres in the quality of the paint and though it was not just a "mere fill-in between lines" there was no substantial structural feeling. She attributed its appeal to its "photographic, expressive, representative value." I disagreed until I covered its face and saw the rest and realized that Violette is correct. It may be the decorative shine of silks and taffeta, its luminescence that pulls us in, but it is the expressive quality that keeps us there. It is a portrait after all, not a Labyrinthian landscape that keeps you searching every inch of its terrain.[110] It was the Dutch terrain of a Vermeer landscape, *View of Delft*, that Violette praised. For her, it met the requirements for a masterpiece, and she described its color, space composition, patterns, and rhythms in a ten-page Barnesian analysis. For Violette, every part of the painting had a convincing reality because of it subtle glowing structural use of color. She compared the depth, variety of hues, and richness of its "color units" to that of Tintoretto. But it was the blue in the painting she said was indescribable, with its sensuous appeal, due to the "unique quality of the color itself, plus its structural use, plus its mottling with spots of light, its variation in individual tones and hues… the gable roof at the immediate right of the church spire was lighter in tone than on the building with the tower to the left of the church spire; the blue of the trees between the two different blues was yet a third hue; yet in all these blues there was a basic similarity of general tone and all of them used structurally. Blue was used both as light and shadow all over the picture where blue would probably not exist naturally."[111] With her sensitive vision, and clarity of thought, she "painted" it for us just with words.

All Clustered in One Violette

"Barnes in Merion"

   – Frances Pepente Wright, 1977
He glorified this house with Venice-light
And drew an arc from Victoire's blue-wedged air
To an enchanted park, transmuting sight
To prismed richness in an ambiance where
Diversity exists in unity.
As planets, brilliant to themselves in space
Fling vaulted fire across the galaxy,
So splendors interact, within this place.
Here harmony's paradigm, it's gathering force,
True mirror of art's clearest excellence,
Reflects jeweled radiance of her inner source.
Though lightly veiled to save our lesser sense.
In her, wit, wisdom, power, grace are met
All spired and clustered in one Violette.[112]

When Frances Pepente Wright sent the draft of *Barnes in Merion* to Violette's close friend in the Barnes seminar, painter and sculptor Myrna Bloom Marcus, she knew with more work the poem "might be better" but felt the choice of sonnet form she used was especially appropriate for a valentine. There were still months ahead before the next St. Valentine's Day, but for Wright and Marcus, it was obvious that the sacred day was not just on one day in February, but every day they visited the Barnes and listened to Violette, who to them signified the Barnes. Where did the Barnes end and Violette begin? Nowhere, it seems. They were clearly one and the same. The light and luster of the Barnes all spired and clustered in one Violette.

Barnes built the house. Dewey filled it with an educational concept. Violette inhabited it early on, and "through her genius as a teacher did more than anyone else to bring about the realization of Barnes' and Dewey's educational aims; it was because of her uniquely sensitive and insightful application of the ideas to the study of art that their full significance is laid open to understanding."[113] Would we hear their voices as clearly and distinctly today if she had not delivered the message as effectively as she did in her lectures and seminal essays?[114] Living with the Mullen sisters, and having the daily influence of Mary Mullen had to have been extremely beneficial in helping Violette quickly grow to fit the Barnesian cloak. Day by day, Violette absorbed the ideas, theories, and philosophies of James, Dewey, Santayana, and Bosanquet. Whatever lectures Dr. Barnes and Lawrence Buermeyer delivered, Violette eagerly attended. She took copious notes during the 1933 to 1934 lectures on music, by the visiting Russian, Nicolas Nabokoff, a writer and composer with the Ballet Russes in Paris, a cousin of the author Vladimir Nabokov [they spelled their surnames differently], and friend of Igor Stravinsky. Nabokoff lectured on Beethoven as the founder of the school of romantic music.

Educator and art historian Thomas Munro, Violette's teacher when she began her studies at the Barnes, was influenced by the educational theories and philosophy of John Dewey, his mentor at Columbia University. Munro believed in a scientific approach to art, rejecting art as simply the expression of the artist. For him, the morphology of art, the philosophical and scientific way of studying art through its form, structure, and parts was a branch of aesthetics. At least, this was his message in early essays published in the *Journal of the Barnes Foundation*.[115] The three years he taught at the Barnes, he understood the philosophy, but did not apply it consistently. This was a major disappointment to Dr. Barnes, who expressed his extreme dissatisfaction.[116]

To Barnes, Munro's talk on unity was the equivalent of futility. His lecture more an oration, and though free of mistakes it was dull and monotonous. "It was almost metaphysical when, right at hand, were scores of instances to make objective unity apparent to any person not blind and not asleep....What was said about *The Music Lesson* was mere patter that never got anywhere near the objective facts which any person could show in a few moments.... On three separate occasions, different pupils demonstrated that what the teacher sought recondite and metaphysical explanations for, could be simply explained by reference to design as I described it to them last week."[117] Munro merely reiterated sections from the books without developing his lesson from direct experience with the paintings. Comments by several of Munro's students revealed that they were more aware than the teacher whose eyes had not yet started to open. This is what Barnes had observed. "The pupils have learned nothing about pictures because the teacher never learned about them himself in terms of experience."[118] Munro's method was "far removed from the method of philosophy we believe in, or with intelligent teaching, living or taking advantage of opportunities offered."[119]

Munro did, in fact, have the ability and skill to pull it together, and demonstrated this in one session in March of 1927. Barnes had walked into the gallery five minutes after Munro had left the class, and "every once in a while one of the six [students] would hover around as if he or she wanted to talk" to him. Eventually, one came over—who happened also to be an employee of Barnes—and told Barnes that "never since they had been coming to the Thursday class had they ever heard such a good, connected, fruitful presentation of both the psychological and the plastic ends of the subject." The doctor asked why that class had been particularly good when it represented the precise method and intentions for all the previous classes. The response was that "no previous class had been anything like this one." The model was there for Munro to see for he had the opportunity to watch Barnes apply the scientific method of teaching many times in the advanced class, and in later years he would write that the Barnes Foundation provided "an invaluable opportunity to learn something about art, aesthetics, and the philosophy of life from these two great, though very different teachers" — Dewey and Barnes.[120] It is likely that one of the "hovering" students who approached Dr. Barnes was Violette herself.[121]

When Violette arrived at the Barnes to tutor French, she already had teaching experience, and cultivation in the arts. She appeared to have the magic mix of talent and skill—a stroke of good fortune for her and the Barnes. Perhaps she sat through Munro's "particularly good" presentation, and noted its value as a paradigm for teaching the Barnesian method. Violette was already an experienced teacher, and attended lectures she heard at the Barnes. Adapting the model for her use as a lecturer at the Barnes would not be difficult.

The brand new Barnes Foundation Gallery was dedicated on March 19, 1925.[122] By the middle of September of that year, Myrton A. Bryant, the President of the Bryant Teachers Bureau and manager of his Academic department, wrote to Dr. Barnes at his office on 40th & Filbert Streets to reiterate his "confidence in Mlle. de Mazia," and to thank Barnes for the opportunity of assisting him in filling the teaching position.[123] From the start, Violette was being considered a candidate for a teaching position—as a teacher of French to several ladies. Art appreciation was soon added.

Violette went to the gallery every day during the week to study. She totally committed herself to learning, and made quite an impression. Within a year she herself was teaching there. As Ross L. Mitchell expressed: "She was thrown into the circumstances through coincidence, but obviously made herself available, and her natural capabilities came to the surface."[124] She may have been provisionally hired for the language-teaching position, but she literally poured herself into the Barnes Foundation and proved her worth early on. It may simply have been a part of her nature. No doubt she truly realized that this special collection of art, in a newly constructed two-story palatial limestone gallery was an extraordinary creation, and posed a unique opportunity like none other. Obviously she had something of great value to give to this place as well. Always interested in art, she fit well in this palatial edifice. She was accustomed to musical soirees being held at her home, so those at the Barnes must have made her feel at home. Able to bridge both music and painting, she could easily take the terminology of one and apply it metaphorically to the other. She did this successfully even in one her earliest essays; specifically, one in which she parallelled a Matisse painting to the music of Stravinsky.[125] It was a new way of looking and talking about a work of art, and she could help to develop this unique approach to the appreciation of art at the Barnes. Her gift with language, in writing and speaking, would enable the teaching of the Barnesian philosophy to thousands of future students.

Violette was immensely grateful for the opportunity that Dr. Barnes had given her. In September of 1926, she wrote to him—in French— from her Fellows Road home in London just before departing for the United States to begin her teaching career there:[126]

> I relish the idea of solitude in which every minute will be filled with visions and revisions in which my memory has been so pleasantly charged. It seems to me I have completely lost the ability to be bored— which I see, of course—as a rare and precious gift. I know who I am indebted to for this 'New World' in which I live now, and I do not thank you just to thank you, because I feel that I shall always be grateful to you without ever having to make a point of it. My parents are not rejoicing at my upcoming departure, especially since I spent very little time with them, and if I didn't love America, and if life were not so good there, I would not have disappointed them and been insistent upon returning so quickly.

A storm in her life initiated the series of events that brought her to Philadelphia, and to the Barnes. She may not have succeeded as an artist in England, but she had a passion for art, and was gifted with all the skills that would make her the ideal teacher, researcher, and writer for Dr. Barnes: the right person in the right place, at the right time, she made the most of the opportunity.

From the start she would pour herself into her teaching and research, constantly honing her skills, using all her talent, educational background, training, experience, and discipline. She was also literally and figuratively creating a new "family" for herself—in and on a structured and secure foundation. It would be the perfect place for her, as Barnes did not forget those who were loyal to him. His housekeeper, Julia, who lived at the Barnes until her nineties, had a lifetime position, free housing, and pay.[127] Barnes recognized Violette's dedication, her talent in expressing herself, her pedagogical and observational skills. Education was key to the ongoing success of the Foundation and its philosophy. Barnes' passport listed "educator" as his profession, not doctor or scientist. This is how he perceived himself. This is what he valued most.

Violette's dedication to learning was evident from the very start, perhaps more so than Munro's, John Dewey's protégé. Her first contribution was the essay "La Peinture" written in 1927 in French for Paul Guillaume's *Les Arts a Paris*. To its readers in Paris, it must have seemed like a Barnesian manifesto:[128]

> A painting? A painting is a totality and it is unique. A canvas coated with color becomes a work of art, only there, where the elements available to the painter are arranged in such a way that it results in communication from the artist to the viewer, communicating her distinctive personal conception of some lived or

imagined experience. Her means of expression are not through other spheres of life: literature, photography, morality, each aimed at a completely different result from that of pictorial art and cannot provide the necessary language for the painter. She conveys her message directly, without any appeal to some intermediary agent, without borrowing from others: She speaks her own dialect, and her vocabulary consists of the plastic elements, that is to say, color, line, light, space, with their countless permutations and relationships. And we have reached this second conclusion, which absolutely does not acknowledge any other intelligent method of studying painting which directly addresses pictorial qualities, skilled "art" [*plastiques*] in the sense that they can acquire different aspects, different characteristics, by changes brought about by their relationships. Synthesis, fusion of these elements into a harmonious whole becomes "plastic form" ['forme plastique' (work of art)] and it is there that it is resolved, constituting and expressing the vision of the painter, her reaction to some object or situation in life, and by which are revealed the qualities of human interest [values] that have struck her imagination. This admitted, it becomes obvious that the first desideratum of a great painter must be to have something to say.

To have something to say is to be in tune with human life, is to be sensitive to the essential values that it contains: but, for that expression, the work of art, to reach a level worthy of Art, she must reveal something of her personal character—the echo of a song, plagiarism of an idea, rehashed, is far from offering the distinctive individuality, charm and flavor of the original model. The criterion based on the individuality of the artist, as well as ownership of the chosen terms, is a fixed standard to which extent modern and ancient art—from all the ages—must be compared. It's not just pretending to appreciate and understand Titian and Michelangelo. If at the same time, one declares oneself unable to recognize the use of the very same traditions in the modern artists, in Renoir, in Cezanne; if we admire the works of the cubists and do not recognize a design analogous to some primitives of Cologne; if an appreciation of Eastern and Greco-primitive art does not lead us into that of the modern Picasso and Matisse we can honestly say we are naive dupes of our own illusions.

The definition of the term *forme plastique* [aesthetic or art form], we deduce by all the possible means,—color, line, space, light—under the brush of the artist, becomes a malleable thing: that is to say, capable of acquiring a different appearance from that which our partial interest in our daily contact with nature has accustomed us. A simplification, an alteration consciously made to the original form of an object is clear and sufficient evidence of a different purpose than photographically reproducing the characteristics of the objects that surround us. The ultimate purpose is the creation of a work of art embodying the personal vision of the artist. In Andrea del Castagno, in Michelangelo, among El Greco, Rubens and many others, isn't it obvious that is their purpose, their artistic intention relates with much more emphasis on an aesthetic form and expressive performance as a rendering of the external world than the black and white photograph on the retina or lens? A painting is an argument: The artist lives, reacts, selects, expresses, and her work becomes the justification of her feelings.

Violette wrote about painting as though through the eyes of an artist. Dr. Barnes, a man of science, wrote more like a scientist, adapting the nomenclature of science into a powerful new method of looking, talking and writing about art. It was a "picking to pieces," and a "reunification of the pieces in a form representing an appraisal of values.... Only as each constituent part is isolated and examined for what it is in itself, [could] its fitness to the whole be determined."[129] Not a mere "dissection" but a knowing of the parts separately and how they fit together as a whole as applied to works of art was a novel and apperceptive approach. The viewer became an active and objective observer, the work of art scrutinized, examined, studied with care. The work of art itself was the source of knowledge. It was the antithesis of how art history was taught at the college and university level, where students were basically limited to parroting back the classroom lecture.

Bob London, a student and devotee of Violette's at the Barnes from 1956 to 1958, described the "established route for an Art History major" at the University of Pennsylvania at that time. "I could identify scores of reproductions and parrot back the important "Five W's" that had been stressed in the slide lectures. These were, 1) Who? 2) What? 3) Where? 4) When? and 5) Why?" London gave an example of what was stressed as important about a particular painting: "1. Pierre August

Renoir (Artist) 2. *Dancers at Bougival* (Given name of picture) 3. France (origin), or Museum of Fine Arts Boston (location) 4. 1883 (date painted) 5. Impressionistic, bright color, happy subjects dancing in an open air café." He developed lists of facts about paintings, sculpture and architecture, but it was never about knowing the painting itself—nothing to do with the appreciation of art. It was not until he was a student at the Barnes that he realized the importance of having the original works of art from which to study. The method of teaching at the university—textbook photos, reproductions, and images from "the incandescent light of a slide projector"—thwarted the possibility.[130]

Knowing a work of art in the Barnesian way differs from the academic, lifeless way Art History had been taught at colleges and universities. The aesthetic experience was a process, not something preexisting and predetermined before the viewer's own experience of it. It was not unlike a physician coming to a patient with a certain knowledge that would help him examine with objectivity, but bring to it the experience with the individual patient that ultimately determined what the doctor would know about the patient. Such it was with art as well.

Thus the door was open to a new way of seeing, with individuals bringing their own unique background and experience with them. Violette brought her own special gift to the brew of Dewey, Barnes, Mullen, Buermeyer—turning their original ideas and viewpoints into classroom practice. She could see what others could not easily see, and verbalize it in a Barnesian way. There is a story that Angelo Pinto, one of the Barnes teachers, shared with his class. One day, as he was sitting in on a series of lectures on Renoir given by

Violette, Dr. Barnes stood up to point out that Violette had said something in the lecture that he hadn't known before.[131]

Violette's earliest observations show a quick learner. As she gained experience, she compared and contrasted artists' works. After she studied the color ensemble of a page from the 12th century Winchester Bible, she pointed out to Dr. Barnes a similar color scheme in Jean Fouquet, but added that it was "very much more miniature-like, more delicate in execution," and the color more appealing.[132] The prevalence of yellowish ivory and a similar linear pattern in François Clouet's *Jean Babou, Seigneur de la Bourdaisiere* reminded her of Ludwig Tom Ring.[133] The landscape in the left panel of the *Resurrection of Lazarus* by Nicolas Fromont of Avignon seemed to Violette a literal representation of the Flemish or German landscape of Jan van Eyck's *Ghent Altarpiece*, and lacked the "lightness and delicacy of the color scheme of the picture in the Louvre.[134]

Observing the woman holding the dead Christ's hands in the 14th century painting *Mise Au Tombeau* at the Louvre, Violette felt Benozzo Gozzoli in the color and pattern of white upon pinkish flesh, and in the relationship of the color to the linear drawing.[135] She observed a color scheme nearly reproducing that of a miniature. To her, it seemed more Italian than French in many places, especially the kneeling white bearded figure in the foreground, where the colors were not limited just to red, gold, old rose, some yellow, light blue, and ivory. The picture shone, glowed, shimmered, with an effulgence comparable to the 13th and 14th century French illuminated manuscripts.

Violette's initial notes at the Louvre above are thoughtful and show complete engagement with the plastic qualities of the pictures she is studying. On her other visits, perhaps rushed for time, she would record details of a work of art, noting the lines, the colors, and shapes with nouns and adjectives with nary a verb—more like free verse. Violette wrote these notes as she observed 11th century frescoes, in a church crypt in St. Savin by candlelight. If we wanted to give the poetic expression a title, it could simply be "Line, Light, Color, Space".[136]

Pear shape faces
Mask like face
Line for features
Nose drawn by lines:
Line from nose on upper lip.
White line over eyebrows.
Rouge on cheeks, not circular like Pernes.
Large head, normal body and puny legs.
Flat background: yellow, blue, white
All enclosing curve in figures.
Parallel lines of three colors and white for folds.
Rosy tan flesh—no shadows, no space
Distorted figure in wheel...

Though these observations were transformed into formal prose in the Barnes publication, *The French Primitives*, Violette's early notes on the lines of the Romanesque fresco are themselves filled with a special energy and movement. Violette observed a work of art, and quickly drew what she saw with metaphors, analogies, and comparisons.[137] The technique was evident even during Violette's interviews of prospective students in the later years, when she felt pressed to accept a huge number of students each year (in proportion to the size of the galleries) and interviews were limited to ten minutes each, with appointments scheduled for several hours each day during the summer months. She quickly limned verbal "sketches," occasionally accompanied by caricatures, or doodle-like drawings of her interviewees. This would not seem necessary for someone with a superb memory, but such mnemonic techniques may have been a necessity when interviewing five hundred to a thousand prospective students annually.[138]

A Voice Akin to a Musical Instrument

With her unique and authoritative voice, Violette delivered long and engaging lectures with confidence, always focused and relevant, yet reserved, drawing out diphthongs, as much keeping distance as inviting. She reached everyone, and was aware of everyone, yet her voice seemed from afar. "She was very soft spoken. But when she wanted to get her point across, she was extremely forceful."[139]

Rachel Sterrenberg, an opera singer and music scholar trained at the Curtis Institute of Music studied Violette's voice from an old tape recording of her lectures. Violette had perfected the Barnesian method to the degree that not only could she write it, and teach it, she was able to speak it as well. She lectured in a unique and distinctive voice, one so rare that only a scholar of music could describe it properly, for it seemed to her something akin to a musical instrument. Not sharp nor high-pitched, but musical. Moving from word to word, sound by sound in almost a symphonic way, she seemed to transform the gallery into a salon of culture and we her guests were not just sitting there, but we were living in it with her. She included us as if we were part of this world. Her voice was unique, distinctive, and authoritative with varied tones and intonation. It could be likened to that of the oboe with its clear, bright sound and her ability to be very precise and rhythmic, while also producing lyrical and smooth sounds and phrases. The oboe, playing a very important role, leads the symphony orchestra with tuning, before a performance. Violette set the tone for the day, and was truly the leader of those assembled.[140]

Ms. Sterrenberg likened Violette's voice to the late classical period of symphonic and instrumental music because of its precise and clean simplicity, yet complexity in color, rhythm, and quality. And so it seemed the perfect substitute for her voice when she moved her fingers through the air as if conducting Beethoven's *Fifth Symphony* to Cezanne's *Card Players* in one of her famous class presentations. Both the music and her performance were truly dramatic. Violette had a "large palette of rhythms in her speech, including: triplets, quick and varied, 16th and 32nd note speeds, and even used dotted rhythms. Stress and intonation were integral to her way of speech. Accents were very important, and she even spoke about how important this was during her first lecture when talking about "white". She gave examples of how different stresses changed the sentiment of the phrases she spoke. Violette was eminently aware of how important her phrasal structure of speaking was to the success of her lecture.[141]

Using the Barnesian Method, Sterrenberg described Violette's voice in terms of color, light, line, and space: Color: She saw yellows and reds when she listened to Violette. They were bright and clean. Light: She had a true chiaroscuro in her vocal color and speech. She used light and dark to explain whatever she was speaking about at all times. This was achieved through changes in intonation, accent, and tempo.

Line: Violette had wondrous skill in speaking with long, varied phrases, with a clear climactic point. Within these long lines, there were accents that were used thoughtfully, with angular personality. Space: There was barely any "unused" space within the art of her speech. She spoke with dense content, no matter what the subject was. The texture of her voice within the space of sound also varied. Violette fine-tuned her voice depending on the purpose of the lecture. When speaking about administrative details at the beginning of the lecture, Violette used precise clarity, with an authoritative, angular intonation. It ended up being a bit higher in tonality than when she spoke of the Renoir. Then her voice was in a lower register, and had a more nurturing color and openness in quality. Her voice adjusted like a well-tuned instrument to differences in subject matter. She had the perfect voice for a teacher, the kind that made it easy to transfer information. Like the oboe, it encompassed all sounds, captured all moods, and nourished many souls.[142]

Violette was a performer, like an actor representing a character in theater she made a vocal adjustment depending on what she was talking about. The thoughtful, precise, premeditated way in which she spoke nearly turned the discussion of art into an art form itself.

Violette was the only one in her family not to master a musical instrument, though in point of fact it was her voice that was her instrument. A conductor would know this, and in guiding her would use long sweeping motions to accommodate her clear, long phrases. It was not a "preaching" voice but one of an advocate. It was the perfect voice for a teacher—one who was not only leading the way but showing a way to see.

Orchestrating Her Classes

*V*iolette not only spoke well and taught well, she conducted—one could almost say "governed"—her classes well. Becoming a Barnes student was a process, and the first step was learning the etiquette and protocol. This began with Violette's introductory lecture.

On that first day, Violette would introduce students to the program, establishing the tone and tenor. She spoke of it as a "getting together kind of meeting." It was an orientation, a description of what to expect, and what was expected of them. Not at all what their typical session would be like, for a number of those attending had not yet been officially accepted, and would not know until after class or by mail before the next session. Far more, in fact, than those actually present that day had not been accepted into the class. Violette said a student once told her "the cows were skidding all over town on the tears of those who have not been accepted in the class." She said that some of those tears were hers and the Barnes, in the sense that they would accept all of them if they could. To dispel any "ill feeling" of those temporarily caught in the "in-between," she explained the decision-making process, and how they would determine the final class group.[143]

Violette said it was the same process that any school would go through; that is, to "weigh one person against another, considering each, of course, from our point of interest." But even doing it that way left them with more qualified students that they could accommodate. The final step was to place name cards in a box and randomly choose the maximum number their rooms could accommodate. As of the first session, they could still be interviewing prospective students. Not all the students attending this session would be asked to return the following week. It sounds arbitrary, but as Violette said: "There is always the part played by luck in our lives; sometimes it's good luck, sometimes it's bad luck, and we have to accept it."

The purpose of orientation was to give the students time to become acquainted with the collection, to satisfy their curiosity so they could relax and concentrate on the lecture that would follow. It was also to establish an understanding of what was expected from the students. There were do's and don'ts she shared with them. Simple logistics at first; such as where to and where not to park. The gallery opened at one o'clock, and students had an hour to roam freely through the galleries, to do their own looking, to apply on their own the principles presented in Violette's previous lectures to any painting or paintings of their own choice. During this time, she would be available for any questions a student might have. Serious work on their own was expected.

From the beginning, Violette firmly stated that the Barnes Foundation was not created merely for the purpose of viewing a collection; nor was it just a place where lectures were given. She explained the rationale for the selection and arrangement of the works of art—the *ensembles* as they are referred to— and how everything that constituted the Barnes Foundation's collection had been carefully planned and carried out. She explained the correlation between the collection, their books, and the lectures. And there were plenty of rules that had to do with behavioral expectations, and discipline: punctuality, attendance, taboos: no photography, no sketching with ink or paint, no smoking; no touching, leaning on or sitting on benches or chairs, no feeling or touching of pictures, nor raising or lowering of shades. If you needed a light on or a shade pulled up, you were to ask Violette, or her attendant.[144] For the protection of the paintings, panels, and other art objects, Violette asked that when they entered the gallery, to keep the front door open for the briefest amount of time. The gallery, she explained, was air-conditioned for the sake of maintaining a constant amount of moisture in the atmosphere so that the canvases and the panels were better preserved. Previously moisture had taken a toll on the art collection. Violette recalled the large canvas of the Seurat "hanging way down like a bag. On other days it became as taut—as taut as a drum; obviously the danger to the paint, to the picture." Panels warped with humidity, and with severe dryness there was danger of wood panels cracking.

On the dark, wintry days that class was held, they had to resort to electric light. Students were asked not to turn the light on when it wasn't necessary, and to ask the teachers or the gallery attendant's permission. The reason being that artificial light changed the color of the painting, and in Violette's terms: "destroyed its identity." Students were also instructed to curb the temptation to stroll on the grounds, as they were also "material for instruction in the various classes of the arboretum." Though these rules seem arbitrary, there was a reason. She wanted them to learn that this was an educational institution, a place of learning, not a museum, nor a gallery.

She described their present course of study, which was a two-year commitment. The first year covered the fundamentals or basic principles of the Barnesian method. The second year was the study of traditions from the early days to the present. In all of the classes, Dr. Barnes' *The Art in Painting* was their guide. The students were required to have their own personal copy, not one from a brother, a sister, or a roommate, nor from a library. They wanted each one to own a copy, so there would be no excuse for not having done the required reading. Their own book with their name and address written in ink on the flyleaf page was their passport to the first lecture in the Foundation. It was the Doctor's rule, and she preserved the custom. The Foundation sold *The Art in Painting* to the students for less than the retail price. You could pay it off ten cents at a time, or with the exact amount to the penny, but she did not want the hassle of "making change." That would be a huge waste of class time.

The seminar was basically a lecture, and Violette did not stop to ask if there were any questions. If someone raised their hand, she would probably have called on them, but to my knowledge no one raised their hand in the Barnes seminar of 1962–1963 that I attended. She said that questions were welcome, "provided that they are pertinent…that they bear on the matter discussed during the classes, and that they be of a nature to benefit the group as a whole." She did not want a student to monopolize the situation. She wanted anyone who wanted to ask a question to wait until they had it formulated clearly. This directive would put a damper on extraneous questions. She called this heckling, a waste of time that interferes with serious work.

On the other hand, It didn't matter if a student never asked a question. She understood that even the very best students might be too shy to express their thoughts in public. "Not to ask questions is not an index of dullness, or of lack of interest. Some very alert, intelligent people, keenly interested, are simply inhibited by their psychological makeup and for the life of theirs, cannot utter a word, or cannot put in words, their thoughts in public, or spontaneously word their thoughts in public." She said that some of her best students fell into that category.

A Melina Mercouri, a Fifi D'Orsay

Though an interview with Violette de Mazia in 1962 was brief, it never seem rushed in any way. There was an intensity, a deep concentration in her look, as though she were seriously studying the interviewee. There was a tranquility about her as well. Her detailed notes from 1970 to 1977 reveal Violette's skill at observation when she literally had only ten- to fifteen-minute interviews with each student.

Violette had a photographic memory, for names and phrases, but since she had to interview many hundreds of applicants every year, she devised a method to keep them straight. Sometimes she drew doodles of them; noting specific details but generally "sketching" the interviewees in the broadest sense with imagistic terms and phrases in this manner: long-faced Dora, tufted brows, round-shouldered, dark under lid, very small mouth, mouth moves to left, black dyed hair, white wavy hair, pearly blue eyelids, plump, low forehead, black pixie, teased salt and pepper, long blond shorter at sides, bouffant whitish blond, bosomy, wiglike, long hair, flattish face, frizzy hair, bony face and jaw, crooked mouth, lavender blue dress and matching eyes, Hindu pose, small nose, shortish, bushy eyebrows, rosy baby face, blonde by choice, sad face, pigeon-toed, Greek profile, Melina Mercouri, long loose knot at back, shoe-button eyes, mouth not centered, Morse code eyebrows, long nails salmon varnish, tip nose dimple, simple country type, thyroid eyes, thick lenses, Indian Madonna, seashore hair, rabbit teeth almost white, thick makeup, dark strawberry French curls, Fifi D'Orsay, young lawyer type, bubbly lips, gaunt pointed face, feline face, Melina Mercouri, and one woman simply described as *vieille* or old woman.[145]

Much was discussed during interviews: background, school attended, career, interest and background in art…. How they came to know about the Barnes, and their reasons for wanting to attend.

Violette was able to delve deeply into the mind of the applicant even with a brief interview. With her keen powers of observation, she astutely observed of one applicant that her "quiet manner belied a keen interest in the world around her." She put everything together, the letters of recommendation, the individual's educational background, and the person's presentation of self: by their dress, way of speaking and interacting.[146]

Violette remembered her students, and it was not just skin-deep. It didn't matter how big the classes became, and they were nearly wall-to-wall in the main gallery in later years. Richard Segal believed it to be, at least partly, a defense against all the attacks that were coming in. She was so determined that people would see it as a school that she added more and more students. "In the last years she was teaching, there were like 120, ridiculous numbers, and she would interview all these people—10-minute interviews—and in September she knew everyone by name. She was famous for that. But she didn't just know them by name, she would remember things about their manner, what they said and even remember what they were wearing, if it was at all unusual. She had a personal interest in each student."[147]

There were ninety-three students in the First Year Seminar of 1962–1963 at the Barnes.[148] Paul Todd Makler, Jr. was a sixteen-year old high school student at the time and probably the youngest who ever attended Violette's course. He still has mental images of Violette, but is not sure if he is conflating two great women into one. To him, de Mazia was so much like his image of Stella Kramrisch, a brilliant art historian of the same era (but with a different specialty). Though many decades have past since his student days at the Foundation, it is obvious Makler can still aptly and easily apply the Barnesian method to a work of art. Line, light, color, space has been etched in his soul. He sees its usefulness, and he perceives its limitations as well.

"Time stopped for Violette,' he said. "Violette was frozen in time." In a way, time did stop for Violette. The same lectures repeated every year, the same process…people came for this, and this was what they expected, and it was a fantastic performance.

Maybe this was true with her class presentations, but she was also very up-to-date with the art world. Even Todd's father, Dr. Makler, Sr. knew this. "Violette was a very impressive teacher with a ridiculously excellent eye. Anything she had ever seen, she remembered." Makler, Sr. had just bought a painting by the artist Justin McCarthy in Philadelphia for twenty-five dollars. "Neither he nor the painting was famous," said Dr. Makler. He could not recall what its subject was, but once when Miss de Mazia came to their home for dinner and saw the painting she said, "I know that painting. I saw it in the Pyramid Club in Washington some years ago. And we took it down and looked on the back, and there was this label. She had that kind of visual memory. It was freakish."

There was one unchangeable requirement at the Barnes. You had to have your own copy of *The Art in Painting.* Hope Seitchik grew up in Merion, right round the corner from the Barnes Foundation, and though she knew about the art collection, she did not know, until she was older, that it was also an educational institution that held classes. She thought it was remarkable that you didn't have to pay anything to attend. Attendance at all the sessions was mandatory, as was a copy of Barnes' book. These were absolute requirements. And, of course, Hope purchased a copy. When her husband, Dr. Seitchik, attended the Barnes soon after her, "ever the thrifty person," she wanted him to use her books. Violette said "no," every student had to have his or her own books. When you purchased the book, you signed your name on the flyleaf, and that was your passport to class.

"Violette," Hope said, "spoke rapidly, concisely, expressively. When she described a painting, I could never get it all down. I never could take the notes that I thought were any good, because you just couldn't take it all in. In fact, when I was so busy writing, I would lose track of the momentum of what she was saying. So I took less notes as time went on and just listened to her and tried to absorb it. In those days, I remembered everything she said. Now, looking back, I have the essence of those years."[149]

"Violette wasn't physically beautiful," adds Hope, "but she was coquettish, charming, charismatic and unforgettable. She was little, but her spirit and everything about her was huge. She was dominant." Even when Hope was talking to her socially, she always felt she had to watch her words because Violette was taking it all in. It wasn't a casual back and forth conversation. She was analyzing you as much as she would a painting.

Violette's way of looking could apply to almost everything in life. Hope agrees. Did Violette's teaching and the Barnesian experience affect the way she looks at things in every day life? "Oh, I think everything," Hope responds, "When I was in New York, I went to design school, which was far away—far, far, far away from what I had done at Penn. I went at night, because I had little children. And I did, it took me three years, but I finished. And so in the work that I did, I was very conscious of putting all the things we learned, like color and space together, and whether I drew a room or whether I placed objects, always a relationship with one thing to another…. Much more so, visually, than when I started that course. No question, it has changed my life in many, many ways."

Hope and her husband took the second-year seminar with Biagio Pinto, and thought he was good. But with Violette, they felt it was different. "Her presence changed the room." Even Violette's "costume" of the day, its color or design or something else, could be significant and reflect what she was going to be talking about. She was, at times, the first clue, and key to the lecture of the day.

Socially, they knew Violette well. Out of the classroom, Violette was a different person. She was lighthearted with a good sense of humor. It was her behavior, the way she carried herself, her deportment that augmented her. "Her face lit up, and she was very expressive," said Hope, who thoroughly enjoyed her social encounters with Violette. "She always brought a new dimension to whatever we talked about."

"Was she easy to be around?" I asked.

"I think she was very easy—I never found her hard to talk to. She loved men—she loved my mother, she loved my father—she adored my husband, more than me, I am sure.... And I think she did like men—liked men in the class. Loved husbands and wives to go together.

"I don't think she was friendly with everybody. I think she was certainly with the teachers. Socially, I don't know if she was friendly with them. I don't know how to say what completion she felt by being there. But, obviously, it was her whole world."

At the Barnes, she was very much at home. "And you certainly got the impression that she was the Barnes...if she was looking for welcoming arms to hold her as part of itself, the Barnes did that. The paintings were her family. The artists were her family. After all, she knew a lot of these artists. That means a great deal than just having art that you are looking at. She knew their life, she had been with them, visited their studios. That became the most important part of her life."

Dr. Seitchik thought of her as a person of mystery. "There were so many layers to learning about her...when she was in class, she did not give any background of herself. She was only there to talk about the paintings. Many of her speeches and lectures were conversational. You usually bring some of yourself in, but she never did that."

Fanny de Mazia, c. 1910, Violette de Mazia Collection, Barnes Foundation.

George de Mazia, c. 1896, collection of her niece, Celeste de Mazia.

Fanny and George de Mazia, c.1897, collection of her niece, Celeste de Mazia.

Feige [Fanny] Fraenkel Mazia with son George and daughter Violette, 1898, collection of her niece, Celeste de Mazia.

Jules Sonny, Fanny, George and Violette, c.1899, Paris, France, Violette de Mazia Collection, Barnes Foundation.

Violette de Mazia, c. 1910, Paris, France, Violette de Mazia Collection, Barnes Foundation.

Violette de Mazia with her brother George, c. 1914, Violette de Mazia Collection, Barnes Foundation.

Portrait of Fanny de Mazia painted by Violette de Mazia, c. 1918, Violette de Mazia Collection, Barnes Foundation.

Joseph Catz, November 1923, Violette de Mazia Collection, Barnes Foundation.

Joseph Catz, November 1923, Violette de Mazia Collection, Barnes Foundation.

Abu Sueir, Royal Air Force Base, 1923, Violette de Mazia Collection, Barnes Foundation.

Class at the Barnes Foundation, 1942. Violette de Mazia is the third person to the right of Dr. Albert C. Barnes, Violette de Mazia Collection, Barnes Foundation.

Sketch of Violette de Mazia teaching her class in Gallery 2, date unknown; El Greco's *Apparition of the Virgin and Child to Saint Hyacinth* on the left, and Cezanne's *The Allee of Chestnut Trees at the Jas de Bouffan* on the right. The marker above her head directs our eyes toward her, and that may very well have been its purpose. Violette de Mazia Collection, Barnes Foundation.

Violette de Mazia, Barton Church, Laurence Buermeyer, and Angelo Pinto, observing Edouard Manet's Laundry (*Le Linge*) in Gallery 2 at the Barnes Foundation, c. 1960s, from the collection of Bob and Sandy London.

Salute to Super Achievers Gala, Juvenile Diabetes Foundation, May 6, 1978, Violette de Mazia Collection, Barnes Foundation.

Violette de Mazia addressing the class at Ker-Feal (Dr. Barnes's farmhouse in Chester County, Pa). May 19, 1986, Violette de Mazia Collection, Barnes Foundation.

Violette de Mazia at the entrance of the Barnes Foundation, Merion Station, John Condax, photographer, Violette de Mazia Collection, Barnes Foundation.

A Leavening Sensibility

*A*t sixteen, I regularly drove myself to the Philadelphia art museum, and was familiar with various artists and painters, yet at eighteen when I first listened to Violette's lectures at the Barnes, much seemed new and foreign to me. I recognized the paintings, I knew artists' styles, but looking back I realize I did not fully understand the Barnesian method, nor did I apply it in the way it was intended. I purchased the texts, *The Art in Painting* and *Art and Education*, perused them, but cannot say I absorbed the totality of their approach to seeing the Art in Art. I had spent my freshman year at the Tyler School of Fine Arts, and transferred in the summer to the University of Pennsylvania. As an eighteen-year-old sophomore at the University of Pennsylvania majoring in the History of Art, I was learning from reproductions, textbook photos, and what seemed a slide a minute.

Between a full load of courses at Penn, and Violette's first-year course at Barnes, my weekday schedule was amply filled. I was lucky that my advisor, Dr. John Walker McCoubrey, recognized the Barnes course as independent research. The result was a decent research paper for someone so young and naïve, with sketches and analyses of a number of Cezanne paintings in the collection. I believe I emphasized the concept of "sandwiching" or layering in Cezanne's landscapes. Was it a Barnesian analysis? I do not remember. It was certainly an attempt at one. The Barnes course was eye opening. But if I didn't fully "get it" then, looking back has given it even greater meaning and value. I never forgot the galleries, the paintings, ironwork, and furniture. Permanent in my memory as well was Violette's unique voice, and her walk with the slight sway of a skater on ice. It is in a doctor's report to Albert C. Barnes that I discover Violette had "markedly everted flat feet" and a mild scoliosis. The doctor suggested that Violette "attempt to correct her postural deformity by walking and standing in an exaggerated position with the toes turn[ed] inward." If Violette followed the doctor's advice, it wasn't for long, and it might have caused as many anatomical problems as it solved. Violette instead turned it into something dramatically graceful as well as unique, almost balletic. She was an artist who spoke musically and wrote imagistically. Perhaps we can also say her words became a kind of "libretto" and her performance her masterpiece.[150]

The prolific author, Richard Wattenmaker, was a history of art major at the University of Pennsylvania, and Barnes attendee simultaneously in the 1960's, and observed firsthand the differences in pedagogical methods between the two institutions. Even as a young student, he had the maturity and wisdom to perceive how beneficial the Barnes was and he expressed his gratitude to Violette. "Often I find it virtually impossible to communicate the principles which have been taught at the gallery. Maybe I have not yet mastered any worthwhile, original, or even crystalized ideas about art but now there is definitely a reason for not giving in or becoming complacent about whatever knowledge I might have gained in the past school year. The reason simply is your ability to communicate ideas understandably to a group. Just as the word 'appreciation' is misused and applied in common reference to art so is the meaning of the word 'to teach.' If teaching is communicating knowledge and interest as well as respect for the teacher and subject then the word can be applied to few people employed by schools today. However, the real meaning of teacher is, I believe, simply exemplified in you. Never have the discussions wandered far from the direct topic of the lecture. You never spoke above or below us and it is difficult to believe how you adapted to the class as a group with so many variables and yet stimulated this interest which, of course, is indispensable in learning. I have sat in the class and certainly not received all that you presented but no matter now how little or how much I derived from each individual lecture there is always a feeling of security and that you know precisely the subject and its related topics."[151]

By comparison with Tuesday at the Barnes with Violette, Wattenmaker felt "the classes and teachers at Penn were a void."[152]

Eileen Serxner, a Barnes Foundation docent, said it was the most incredible experience of her lifetime to be a student at Barnes. "I understood when I was there what was happening. I understood that this was a brilliant lady and I was experiencing…once in a lifetime moments. And it was transformative. I mean everybody tells you that. And I would just sit there with my mouth open, and I completely drank the Kool-Aid…And I was hers; I mean I believed whatever she said. There were times when I would question certain things. And I was never afraid actually, to ask her a question. Never. I know people have —I don't know if people have told you, or you had felt that yourself, being intimidated by her, but I never was. Never was. And she was always very respectful of my questions, anyway. Sometimes she had no time for other people's questions—she would tell them to sit down. But yeah, it was—I knew I was in the presence of greatness..."[153]

Serxner did not realize in the beginning that Violette would dress in a special way for the class: there were the Modigliani, the Cezanne, and the Renoir outfits. "I didn't realize until we were talking about surrealism and I believe she wore some kind of crazy belt with a hand to class." It was then she realized Violette's own choice of clothing, jewelry, and flower pinned in her hair was a clue to the art ensemble chosen for the day. It was her way of getting us to look, really see." Violette had a special presence about her and she really controlled whatever was happening in that room. "It was a big room with over a hundred people in it and she was almost a disciplinarian—you couldn't do this and you couldn't do that and you could eat your lunch but... you couldn't use candies that had wrapping paper on it because that made too much noise. She was formidable, very much in control, and she had a real presence about her." [154]

Serxner noted Violette's youthfulness and energy, despite the fact that she was already in her mid-seventies when she was teaching the class: "She never gave in any way the appearance of an old person because she was so full of life. Although she had her throat problems at that point and she was always taking cough medicine and it would be in the middle of a class she would scream out, and an assistant would come running in with the cough medicine for her."[155]

Serxner was Violette's student for ten years, so she saw the change over time of Violette's vitality: "At the beginning she was…full of energy and life and all of that. But I remember one of the last times we were at Ker-Feal, and she usually would hold court there, you know, she would be the hostess. And at this one last time, she just sat on a bench, kind of outside on that porch area, and she just kind of sat by herself very quietly. And then, during that same time, she was taking us on a tour around the house, and she felt faint. And people said just lie down on the bed and she commented that she's really not supposed to lie on these covers because the property was more important than her comfort."

By the time Serxner was her student, Violette had an enormous reputation, and everyone knew how qualified she was to be up there in front of all of them. "So it was first of all a huge respect that everybody had for her…her command of the language and the way she expressed herself and just watching her flutter about, and of course her charm. I mean that French accent—you couldn't help but just be fascinated and mesmerized by her, and that was part of her control."[156]

It was a wintry January, and snow blanketed the spacious woods surrounding the mountain home that Irvin Nahan shares with his wife Polly. "Who in the city would want to ride up here in the snow?" he wondered aloud, but applauded me at the same time. Nahan is an animated speaker, giving all of himself in every breath. You sit there absorbed, not just drinking him in but gulping wave after wave of his vibrant memories of Violette and the Barnes.[157]

In one of the rare breaks in conversation, I hand Nahan a copy of the passenger record from his Barnes-funded trip to Europe the summer of 1953. "How did you get this?" he asks. Nahan had traveled to Europe with artist Barton Church that summer, and was glad to have the copy of the actual record of their travel to Europe and back. "It was de Mazia's decision," he said. His friendship with Church developed at the Barnes. They sat next to each other during Violette's lectures. It was apparent to Nahan that Church seemed to understand what de Mazia was saying. "I loved it, but I didn't understand it and I would ask Church questions and we developed this friendship." Violette, he said, realized Church's intelligence. Nahan remembered Church calling him to say de Mazia had come to his studio and asked him to become a teacher at the Barnes. "It was perfect for him and the Foundation." This was a couple years after Dr. Barnes himself had seen a painting of Barton's that the artist wanted to give to Violette. When Barnes saw it, he bought it, and *Girl in a Chair* remains part of the Foundation collection.[158]

Nahan and Church would share their work with each other, and encouraged each other. One day when Violette was visiting Church's studio, she admired some of Nahan's little drawings. On that very day, Church said to Nahan that he would like to take de Mazia out to "a real Greek restaurant on Spruce Street," and wanted Nahan to "come along." Nahan never forgot what Violette was like that night: "…she enjoyed herself…she was so at ease. There was a waiter there who seemed rather shy and stuffy, but he must have been a very good-looking man, and she made comments about how good looking he was, and she was open about it too. Not that she ran around bragging about her sexuality or whatever… she was just telling me that there was so much about her other than being this wonderful teacher…like a sensualist who was very aware of life's sensuality and expressed it in a very acceptable way—about pictures—how alive she was to the qualities that made a picture wonderful, particularly like you know, Renoir—but without a display."[159]

It was years later, as a mature man that Nahan said he had the wisdom to realize what he could not as a young man about Violette and Barnes; that of the possibility of a "powerful connection" between the Doctor and Violette. "It wasn't insulting to think about that....Why not?" he said.

I agree and offer that it was a meeting of two brilliant minds and she really understood him very well, clearly. And I am sure he appreciated her, for her extreme intelligence and astuteness, and sensuality in terms of appreciating color, of a *joie de vive* in looking at things, an appreciation of aesthetic things. Researching, writing four books together, they had to have known each other well. They were not naïve, and saw what was really there in the other. And I think it was their combination that made a lot of this thing happen the way it did. Violette, a talented educator, brought superior intellectual skills, photographic memory, a poet's heart and what has been termed a "leavening sensibility" to Barnes' scientific analytic ability. I think it was a miracle, actually, that the two came together. Nahan agreed and wondered what would have happened had they not met. Doubtless there would not have been the same result if Violette had not come to America, to Philadelphia, and answered a newspaper advertisement for a French tutor at the Barnes. "If they didn't meet, you would wonder how these individuals were going to express what they were capable of. It was a miracle," said Nahan.

Nahan saw it as an equal relationship, each bringing something vital and essential to it. Barnes, as analytical as he was, still needed someone who had the capacity, energy, and patience to turn these new ideas into something solid and concrete that people could read. And that was de Mazia who "absolutely loved the language...who loved the ideas" and had the "patience and skill to help and to form those ideas that became the books they wrote. They needed each other equally—one not more than the other. And she loved the process. I think that was essential. Barnes could depend upon her. She not only grasped the ideas that he was so passionate about, but she was able to help incorporate them in lectures that were solid and understandable. She had the patience and the gift for teaching, and empathy for the students who were struggling. Instead of thinking them limited, she saw it as an opportunity and enjoyed it. At times there were students who were helped dramatically without being able to describe just how she did it. This was a slow process. She was open and did not demand the responses immediately."[160]

Rina and Newt Malerman both attended Tyler School of Fine Arts in the 1950s, but did not attend the Barnes class until the 1970s. Rina said: "Barnes wasn't even something you would consider because they were not allowing people like us to go there." [She did not explain why, and I did not press for an answer.] Her sister had started the classes in the late 1950s, then attended the seminars, and became active in Friends of the Barnes. She advised Rina that when she got to the point where should could promise not to miss a class— Rina's children were young at the time—she should apply. She did wait, and when she got to that point, she applied, and was accepted. She would come home and tell Newt how wonderful it was.

"We never had anything like this at Tyler. There was never a discussion of aesthetics, you know, it was always the fundamentals, how you do it, how it's made, and the history of art, but from a very different point of view. Not from an aesthetic point of view.

"And I was just so over the top with it. I was just so thrilled and my artwork changed, you know, all of this is during that period of time. And I came home and I said to Newt, you have to do this. You have to go. So he managed to arrange his very busy schedule." Though he was running a factory, he found the time.

Newt said that when Violette interviewed him, he told her his art education at Tyler had been a "cheat." It had been terrific from a "technique point of view, but as far as the aesthetics [were] concerned...nothing discussed," and that was why he was applying. He had enjoyed his conversation with her then, and others that followed. She enjoyed them as well. "She was very partial to men," said Rina: "First of all, there weren't that many men in the class. There weren't that many men who could manage to leave and be there and you know, dedicated to being there, which you had to be." After completing the second year, if you wanted to continue, you would take the seminar with de Mazia." This was, said Rina, "really a privilege... And if there were any men in the class, she just would defer to them all the time—you could just see it; she just loved having a man in the class. And she'd do a little flirting...." I asked if that made them respond in a different way. Did it make them feel special? Newt said, "Yeah, she was much less stern with men than she was with women. She had a good time with men." Rina added: "She did. It was charming." "To be a student of de Mazia," said Newt, "was incredible. She was very precise with what she taught. And always with a good deal of humor, I felt. Certainly kept us on the edge of our seats frequently."

The second year "seminar was a joy...she said very little but I suddenly realized how simpatico she was. It was my turn to give a seminar speech. And I took a chance and I decided to take a canvas that I had and just splatter it with paint. And I brought it in and my—what's his name? Tom Wolfe had written book called *The Written Word* which had to do with the importance of the word in contemporary art at that time, which he felt was not art at all.

"So, I did this canvas which was not art at all, and I covered it with a veil. First you had to deliver the speech to a small committee and Miss de Mazia, and if they approved it, then you gave it to the whole group. She came in early and she looked and she said, "May I take the veil off? So I said yes. She took the veil off and she looked at the piece and she looked at me with that sly little grin." She caught on immediately and published Newt's speech.

It was a feast at their home that was most memorable to Rina. Newt had worked in Hong Kong and loved the food but couldn't find anything like that here. In northeast Philadelphia, he located a Chinese restaurant that served real Chinese food—not chow mein. It was a family-owned restaurant: the husband was the *maître d'hôtel*, the wife was a Shanghai-trained chef, and the daughter was the waitress. Newt convinced them to open a cooking school and there he learned how to cook authentic Chinese food. About a year later, the Malermans invited Miss de Mazia to their home for a Chinese banquet. Newt chauffeured her back and forth. It took weeks to prepare the 20-course banquet. "It's a long time in preparation, and it was exquisite," said Rina.

That special night, Violette sat next to Newt, and as she tasted the food she would tell him what it was. "She hit the nail on the head except for one spice that I used; she told me every single ingredient that was in there. It was an amazing tour de force." Violette had never been to Asia, how and where would she have picked up this skill and knowledge? Newt simply said it was her "refined senses." Did her early experience in Paris, and Brussels train and educate that sophisticated palate, so that she could identify just about every seasoning used? There was just a short jump from palate to palette, and identifying the myriad colors of a painting. Her skill at one would equal the skill of the other and her refined and educated senses were as exquisite as the feast itself.

This awareness and artistic fluidity reminded Rina of Violette's analogizing a Cezanne painting to the music of Beethoven. She hums "Da-da-da-dum" to the entry bars of the Fifth Symphony. I tell her that I remembered Violette conducting Beethoven's Fifth to the Cezanne *Card Players* in the main gallery, but I did not recall actual music. Rina said when she heard Violette's presentation there was music: "She had the phonograph there, she had the record there, and she played that. And as she played it, she pointed to each tree in the Cezanne painting. I mean, whoa! That was just fabulous."

"It was theatre," added Newt.[161]

Richard Segal considered Dr. Barnes and de Mazia a harmonious pairing. "She was a true partner to Barnes. The Barnes Foundation that I experienced would not have existed if it weren't for her. When people spoke about the Barnes course and how it transformed their lives, as so many people did, they were talking about the de Mazia course. Barnes did not teach at the Foundation except for an impromptu talk now and then. She designed that course completely herself. I mean that was a unique and original creation with each lecture a work of art itself. And they built one upon the other in a symphonic form. And the whole thing was this majestic picture that was unlike anything anywhere. And it was her creation."[162]

It is questionable whether the Barnes course in Art Appreciation would exist today if Violette had not collected the notes from her class lectures, then revised, edited, and published them in the 1970s, with the assistance of her associate editor, Ellen Pyle Homsey. For this purpose, she established the VOLN Press. Spoken as the V-O-L-N Press, with each letter pronounced separately, it identified and merged the given names of the two editors: Violette and Ellen.[163] When I discovered the meaning and significance of the acronym, it confirmed my intuitive feeling about Violette. She was anything but self-serving, and felt no need to enhance her self-esteem. It was the work itself that counted, and how helpful it would be to the Barnes.

Ellen Pyle Homsey had driven the fifty miles to Segal's home in Merion from Delaware to participate in the interview. I had interviewed her sister Margaret Pyle Hassert the week before my meeting with her and Richard Segal. Ellen is a very private person, similar in personality to Violette, and it is only through her sister, Margaret, a very talented editor in her own right, that I discover more about Ellen's dedication to Violette, and Margaret's to her sister. When Ellen was pregnant with her first son, she had a tendency to faint. Obviously, it would not be safe for her to drive the long distance alone. Her sister Margaret chauffeured her each morning to Violette's home in Merion Station, stayed with her during the working day, and drove her back home to Delaware, until the issue was ready to send to the press. There was such a strong bond between the two editors that Violette was named godmother to Ellen's first-born son, Walter.[164]

"More than anyone I have ever known," Segal said, Violette "had the left brain, the right brain working totally in sync, in harmony, crossing back and forth with total ease. She had the mind of an artist, she had the mind of a poet…she was a great teacher. She really could have been an actress… And she had the ultimate librarian's type of mind—the most organized, mathematical mind, and a feel for language. I've just never known anybody on that level."[165]

During our meeting, Segal asked Homsey what it was like helping Violette refine the lectures, she said: "Well, they were spoken and you needed to translate them to a written form. And it's a difference as you, I am sure, are well aware." "It was more than that," Segal added, "you actually influenced her thinking in many areas…what was it like to work with her?" Homsey is clearly reticent about sharing stories of her closeness to Violette: "That's not a kind of question I can answer. I'm sorry…I'm not good at formulating these responses." Segal said Homsey played a critical role, but Homsey shook her head as if to disagree.

After reading Homsey's brilliantly argued essay on the aesthetics in art, it is evident that she is indeed a masterful writer, brilliant thinker, and was the perfect co-editor for the journal. No doubt Violette knew this. The two editors worked so closely and so well together that the finished product was seamlessly unified. Even the official emblem of their press is the seamless interweaving of their names.[166]

"The Barnes Foundation that I experienced would not have existed if it weren't for Violette," said Richard Segal. "When people spoke about the Barnes course and how it transformed their lives, as so many people did, they were talking about the de Mazia course." Dr. Barnes's teaching was limited to the occasional "impromptu talk." Violette "designed that course completely herself. I mean that was a unique and original creation where each lecture was itself a work of art. And they built one upon the other in a symphonic form. And the whole thing was this majestic picture that was unlike anything anywhere. And it was her creation."[167]

Segal described Violette as a great teacher with the mind of an artist and poet. "She really could have been an actress," and she had the "most organized, mathematical mind... and feel for language." It was her extreme dedication to the Barnes that he recalls. "She was, I guess in her mid-eighties at the time. She was getting something from the basement. She fell down the basement stairs... as she started to fall, she thought this is the end of me. Well, she broke three ribs, and climbed back up the stairs. It was Tuesday. She went to the Foundation, taught her three and a half hours, or almost four hours, of lectures, and then went to the emergency room. That was de Mazia." There would be other times when she would sign herself out of a hospital against doctor's orders, take a taxi to the Barnes, teach her class and then taxi back to the hospital. As Segal said, "It was her life, really."

Cognitively flexible, organized, systematic, creative, and intuitive in equal measures, Violette was just as skilled at thinking and writing metaphorically as writing and thinking in the objective Barnesian way. To do this you have to have both sides of the brain working well. Along with the scientific approach you need poetic imagery. You have to be able to have that kind of fluidity. And it isn't easy for everyone to think this way. Even artists who are gifted at painting might not be as gifted in finding the words to express themselves. Segal gave an example: Barton Church, who he believes to be one of the greatest artists of the second half of the 20th century, would have unusual titles to his paintings. He gave several examples: *Blonde Bombshell*, *Peaceable Kingdom*, and *Lime Juice*. Violette, apparently, was the one who named his paintings. "And they're very imaginative and they just capture what the painting—something intrinsic to the nature of the painting." On the back of the canvas of *Lime Juice*, Church wrote: "To Vio, the only person who can encapsulate a painting in a word." Vio's gift with language seems similar to her gift for detecting all the spices in a dish she was tasting even for the first time, or precisely which blues, greens, yellows, or reds, were in a painting by any particular artist.[168] With equal precision, she could translate paintings into words.

Violette was a gifted speaker, and a multi-linguist, but which language could we say was her native tongue, having left her birthplace of Paris for Brussels at the age of two, and then to London at eighteen? How secure did she feel writing in English, perhaps her fourth language, after French, Italian, and German.[169] Wise and sensible, it is likely that Violette relied on Homsey to edit her essays. As to her influence on Violette's thinking and what it was like to work with her, Homsey remains humble and silent.

Frank Colgan was the sales representative for the company that published Violette de Mazia's journal *Vistas*, and that is how he became connected with the Barnes Foundation for thirty-one years. The account had originally been handled by the man who ran the company, but when "he was up in his years," Colgan took over the account. This was 1961, and he handled it from then on. His first connection was with Mary Mullen, who had visited the plant to see their facilities, and later his connection was with Mildred Winnings, Violette's secretary.

"So then, I went there and, as I said, I worked with Mildred Winnings. She would take all the information from Miss de Mazia and her articles and pass them on to me to be put into typeset form. And then I would bring the galleys back to Mrs. Winnings and back and forth. I didn't really see Miss de Mazia much in the early years. And all my work was at 403 Haywood Road, which was her office. That was close to Waldron Mercy Academy, just off Montgomery Avenue, not far from the gallery. And they had more grandfather clocks in that place than I ever saw before. And I don't know if Dr. Barnes lived there before he moved into the gallery or not, but that was their main office. And most of the place was empty; they only used a few rooms for offices. But I dealt with Mrs. Winnings for years, and then she passed away very suddenly.[170] And I started going directly to Miss de Mazia's home, I guess about eight or nine years, I'm not sure."

The last time Frank saw Violette was a week before she passed away. "She was unforgettable…a very kind person. She was always very good to me. And we got along beautifully. But Violette was very shy." "And formal," I added, and told him a little story about another student who knew Violette for twenty years, and assisted her a great deal during her last days. Violette asked her, after all those years, "may I call you by your first name?" Only then did she address her student informally. The reverse, however, would not have been possible. The student wouldn't think of addressing Miss de Mazia by her given name. Formality in etiquette was the custom. Frank Colgan knew her for a lengthy time as well, but he tells me: "Oh, boy. It was Mr. Colgan for me, and I would never call her Violette. I'd be out the door by then. No. It was always a very pleasant relationship, but not that close."

Frank would bring the galleys to her home on Derwen Road for her to proofread. When they were ready, he would pick them up at the office. When the changes were made, he took them back again to her home. "So I was there many times—always in the living room. But near the end, I would work with her in her bedroom, right by the side of the bed."

"She was a perfectionist," said Lorraine, Frank's wife, who also was a student of Violette's. Frank totally agrees. There were supposed to be two issues a year of *The Journal of the Art Department*, but "she took so long working on them, that sometimes it was more like eight or nine months. And she would make a tremendous amount of corrections. It's like when you're building a house and you decide to move the closet to the other side. They're called alterations. Many times her alterations cost more than the basic setting of the book from the very first. One year it got to be $25,000—just for one of those books. And the Foundation didn't have the money. They said you're going to have to pay for them yourself." This is when Violette began the publication of *Vistas*. Colgan said that on the average, Violette looked at the galley proofs eleven times. Then when it got to the next stage, she looked at the proofs, on average, about seven times, and she would constantly make changes. She would put in a "the" and maybe a month later, she'd take the "the" out. "We always said that if we compared the last set of galleys with the first set, it probably would be identical… It was her perfectionism. And that's just the way she was. It was her money and whatever she wanted to do, we didn't argue with her." Violette even continued to proofread and hone the published work. Though some might interpret this as indecisiveness, I see it as the everlasting moulding of the message toward perfection. How many times does an artist change the painting until it is done? Violette's canvas was the blank page, her pigments were words.

I ask Frank if he saw her art collection while he was there. "Well, it was all over the house." Behind couches too. Typically, they would sit on the couch facing a bank of windows. He remembers Pennsylvania Dutch chests and grandfather clocks in the living room. Paintings hung from the knobs of chests. He even noticed a Renoir painting propped up against a wall—a lady with a hat. He couldn't get over that, so one day, his curiosity got the better of him, and he asked her if it was a real Renoir. She said no, that she bought three copies in 1937 at John Wanamaker's for five dollars apiece, gave two of them away to friends, and kept the remaining copy. Frank was "devastated" because he thought it was an original.

Violette did have reproductions, but they were mainly for teaching purposes. She was a collector, but not of Cezanne, Renoir, Prendergast, Tintoretto, or El Greco. Considering the limited funds she had to purchase art, she purchased wisely and well. Though she probably had an idea of the appraisal value of her collection, she would consider it irrelevant that the Christie auction of her collection of furniture and fine arts grossed nineteen million dollars in 1989. The largest sum the Mazia's estate received for a work of art was one million dollars for the Matisse gouache triptych that the artist gave her. She could not afford a Correggio, but she did have a painting from the Circle of Correggio; not Perugino, but after Perugino; not Angelica Kauffman, but school of Angelica Kauffman: After Francois Boucher, School of Joseph Vernet, School of Gaspard Dughet, Circle of Balthasar Beschey, manner of Albrecht Durer. Of original works by more contemporary artists, she had Georges Braque, Marc Chagall, Joan Miro, Jules Pascin, Wassily Kandinsky, Alexis Gritchenko, Chaim Gross, Salvatore Pinto, Luigi Settanni, Francis McCarthy. She had six works by Jean

Hugo, and eleven works by Abraham Walkowitz. She hung her paintings in the style of the Barnes; that is, in layered wall ensembles. When they were removed for the estate sale, you could see the pattern, exact size and location of each painting because the paint had faded on the wall around the artwork. Besides paintings, she was a collector of porcelain, pewter, and textiles. Considering she was living on a fixed lifetime income of $10,000 per year, she managed to build an impressive collection, not just paintings, but antique pewter, wrought iron, 19th century Staffordshire, and Pennsylvania Dutch textiles.[171]

Violette may not have been there when Dr. Barnes began to build his impressive collection, as were the Mullen sisters, Mary and Nelle. Nelle, who became the president of the Board of Trustees at the Barnes Foundation, seemed to have taken full advantage of Dr. Barnes' offer to sell his paintings to his employees at cost. When Mullen died, the collection of paintings from her estate included eight Renoirs, two Matisses, four Pascins, two Soutines, a Cezanne, five Prendergasts, eight Demuths, seventeen Glackens, two Lawsons, a Utrillo, a Degas, a Rouault, two de Chiricos, and two Signacs.[172]

I am sure Violette was more than familiar with Mullen's collection, but do not know if Violette attended any of the Freeman sessions for her estate. If she had a curiosity as to the market value of works of art, she would never confuse it with its aesthetic value. Seeing what the Mullen estate brought in at the Freeman auction, however, may have spurred her into creating the Violette de Mazia Trust, to enable the Barnes educational method to continue to survive and thrive.

Ebbing Away, Yet Writing Away

By the time Sharon Bloomfield Hicks came to work for Violette, Violette had been a force at the Barnes Foundation for most of her adult life; lectured more than a thousand students, and published journals with her students' essays as well as her own for more than twenty years. Her own twenty-nine essays form the basis of Barnes' seminars to this day.

Hicks grew to know her extremely well. A recent graduate of Tyler School of Fine Arts, she began work as Violette's personal assistant in 1987, and remained with her through de Mazia's illness in the fall of 1988.[173] This experience had a tremendous impact on Hicks because she was very close to Violette during this time, communicating with her everyday: she didn't want to talk to anybody except me because she just didn't feel well." Hicks was overseeing her class, "behind the scenes," during that first year. "Answering all the correspondence and everything from what was going on politically to what was going on with the class to what was going on personally. It was really cool that she trusted me and I was being mentored by her and I didn't even know it."

Violette had her attend the classes at the Barnes so that she could report how they were going. Students would come up to her and tell her the parts of the lecture they thought were especially good that day that really interested them. When she met with de Mazia after class, she would always ask what happened in class? Hicks would tell her. Violette would remember her own talks word for word, write them down for Hicks who would hand them over to whomever was teaching the current seminar. And then a week later she's like, "'No, no, no, that wasn't it, it's this.' And then she wrote it down again. And she would be that way. And she would wake up in the middle of the night, and she always had a pad next to her. And she would write—she would tell me…during the night, or whenever it was, whenever she had the inspiration, she would write it down. And then she would have these pages she would give me and they would be like circled and lines here and there and, you know, where she filled it in and changed it, and then I'd have to go back and type it and bring it to her. And then she would change it again. And that was like so interesting to see how she thought, how her brain worked and how she kept with it until it was the way she wanted it. And she could always change it on any given day, it was never done."[174]

"Violette was very private about herself," said Hicks. "It was always all about the work and nothing else was important." After a celebration of Violette's birthday, Hicks, believing Violette was eighty years old (she was ninety-two!) and that the birthday was either the 10th or 11th of that month, remembered asking Violette on which day her birthday fell. "On both," Violette answered. In actuality, it was neither. Violette may never have seen an official copy of her French birth certificate.

Observant Violette became accustomed to Hicks' wardrobe, and one day asked her to attend the class on Modigliani the next day wearing her purple shirt with the bow. Hicks didn't realize that she was dressed like the model in the painting that was going to be discussed until she was right there in front of it. "It was hysterical," Hicks said, being a kind of "stand in." Hicks had worn the outfit only once since she had begun working there, but Violette remembered it. Though she didn't recall the precise conversation, Violette said she was like a Modigliani.

Violette felt close enough to Hicks to confide in her that it "took everything that she had to do these classes and to get up in front of people." Adding that the same held for those "very social occasions where she felt so uncomfortable sitting next to so-and-so." I told Hicks that this description of Violette really did fit with what I have discovered. Violette seemed to connect well with a certain type of personality: one being her associate editor of the *Vista* journals, Ellen Homsey. Hicks quickly agreed, "a very talented person, very shy." I add that though this is true, Ellen would be quick to correct any inaccuracy she read in an essay or heard in a conversation. She is the ultimate editor. When I interviewed her along with Richard Segal, an outgoing and confident speaker, she would not hesitate to correct him, or supplement with commentary when she thought it appropriate. But she said at the very beginning of our conversation that she was "not a speaker…I'm just too shy for that kind of thing." Violette seemed drawn toward people who were artistic, creative, literary, and reserved.

"Violette was so devoted. That was the biggest thing about her…she was devoted to carrying on the work exactly as Barnes left it…she would always go back to 'this is the way it was when he left…to carry on the work.'" Hicks believes that this may have been the reason why she resisted change—the opening of the galleries to the public for three days a week—because that took time away from her teaching. One change then might lead to another. To someone dedicated to preserving Drs. Barnes' and Dewey's experiment, this seemed perilous. Hicks calls her time with Violette a "work of art"—putting everything into place, making sure everything was sound and secure with the Barnes Foundation. Hicks did a lot of typing, answering phones, talking to students. Everyday, she would go to Violette's house in the morning and in the afternoon. Violette would tell her what to assemble for the current class, and Hicks would gather together what was needed. Eventually, Richard Segal took over the teaching when Violette could no longer do it, but Violette would always ask Hicks how the class went. "She would talk about it a little bit with me."

"You were her eyes and ears," I suggest. "Not that much. She didn't have that much energy, so she was even more selective about what she would say or what was important...I sensed that she could talk a really long time, but she didn't feel well. So every afternoon, I would go and she would sign letters, and if there was a mistake, she would just correct it. She didn't make me type it over, and never said anything to make me feel bad. Like a mentor, she always pushed you to keep being more than you were."

"She had things she really wanted me to know," said Hicks. "I would leave work at quarter of four and go over to her house, which was just around the block. And I wouldn't leave there until five. She would talk for a whole hour. Being on the meek side, I wouldn't say, 'excuse me, I have to go.' Not only that, it was interesting. I just wanted to listen to her because everything she said was meaningful, really important, or she wouldn't be spending the time. It was just really, really great."

When Hicks arrived at de Mazia's stately colonial home on Derwen Avenue in Merion Station the morning of September 20, 1988, she saw that both day- and night-shift nurses were there together in Violette's bedroom. She also noticed Violette's very raspy breathing, but didn't know its full significance. Later she would, of course. Violette knew she felt different. When Violette's physician, Dr. Henry D. Cornman, III called earlier, she told him not to visit—she wasn't up to it and didn't want to see anyone. But that morning, Violette had asked Hicks to stop by the Horn of Plenty store in Narberth to pick up "stuff for salad." Hicks called before going on the errand to see if there was anything else she needed, and the nurse who answered said: "I don't think you need to go. Do you want to come over here, she's taking her last breaths."

The end may have seemed peaceful, but the nurse's log from June to September makes it evident that Violette had her share of chronic pain and discomfort the summer of 1988: Medications and frequent hospitalization for a chest tap for shortness of breath.[175] In mid-June of 1988, her night nurse, K. Philips observed purple areas on her side, her back, and on both inner arms, and weight down to 99 pounds. Violette was "active around [the] clock," nurse Phillips wrote, "… anxiety, very little rest or sleep."[176]

Violette fought hard to live long enough to write down everything of importance; writing everyday with a passionate resolve to tell the story the way it happened, Dr. Barnes' story, her story, the way it was, so we would get it right, and keep it right for posterity.

On September 12th, she had a blood transfusion, and returned home from the hospital the next day. Her friend

Marcelle Pick, a trained nurse, watched her from breakfast to early evening on September 16th and observed that Violette remained lethargic and had a slight tremor. On the 17th, Violette experienced shortness of breath. The night nurse wrote in the medical log on September 18th that Violette had been "Up and down… 100 times." She "never slept for 5 minutes," "I am beat to my socks," Violette told her.[177]

Early afternoon on the 20th, her head drooping, stooping on standing, weak, skin cold, moist to the touch, blood pressure extremely low, Dr. Cornman advised Violette to go to the hospital but she refused.

Violette knew she felt different. She had actually told Cornman not to bother coming to see her that day. That would be atypical of her, but she knew the visit was not going to change anything. One nurse described it simply: "She went to sleep, and her heart stopped." The end seemed to have been peaceful. It had been just a matter of a few hours between her earlier comment to Dr. Cornman and her last breath.

By the time Hicks arrived, Violette was gone. She remembered "going in the other room and crying…I guess it was…expected to happen, at that point…probably could have a lot sooner, but she didn't let it happen. You know, I mean, if you were in a time when you didn't have modern medicine, right, she would have been gone." Even sooner, Hicks implied.

The powder compact that Violette always kept under her pillow had fallen from her bed at the end. Did she in her last waking moments freshen up her face to prepare for the meeting for which she had been waiting decades? Without seeming bizarre, we can imagine whom she hoped to meet— certainly Joe Catz, Dr. Barnes, other loved ones. She was readying herself for the work that might very well be just beginning, and she would be ready.

The compact had been removed from a violet handbag she had by her bed at the end, a Morris Moskowitz creation in jeweled-tone velveteen with black patent leather straps, not quite super-size but large enough to hold a handkerchief with a design of the Fontana di Trevi, World War II ration book, a religious charm of St. Joseph and Baby Jesus, two Le Dauphin leather pocket-size photo albums, one in red, one in black that contained two photos of her mother Fanny Fraenkel de Mazia in front of their home in St. Gilles, Belgium, prior to their leaving at the onset of war in 1914; a view of Port Manech, and a photo of Dr. Barnes' Brittany Spaniel, Fidèle de la Port Manech; one of Violette next to the well in Port Manech that Dr. Barnes brought back to his newly built mansion in Merion Station; and those of deer, a lake, and mountains perhaps from the earliest research trips to Europe for the Barnes. There were the typical items found in a woman's bag: coin purse, mascara, powder compact, Kent of London tortoise comb, even a pink hair curler, and more than a dozen keys: a house key with a needlepoint tag with the name "VIO" in royal blue against a background of baby blue framed in white; another key with a raised design, almost Victorian-looking, perhaps the key to the family home in London. There was a list of important telephone numbers: doctors, closest friends, a fellow trustee, publisher's agent, her nurse, and the name of the Barnes' student she asked to conduct the current Tuesday afternoon class on the rare days she was too ill. It was as if she carried her history with her.

By her side as well were two extravagantly embroidered Brittany bonnets, and a velvet blue and white skullcap embroidered with gold and emblazoned with miniature jet beads. Was she thinking of the fall class that was soon to begin at the Barnes and had these highly ornamental caps on-the-ready to explain the decorative in art? It must have been a force of habit, after all that September in 1988 was her sixty-third year at the Barnes.

Violette remained prepared to the very end; involved and consciously concerned with every lecture to be given at the Barnes. She was the genuine thing, and to the very last breath of her life remained Barnes' most faithful disciple. Every essay she wrote, every lecture she gave was for the Barnes. Her writing nearly every day of her life was itself a perpetual memorial to Dr. Barnes. I remain humbled by the words of Bob London, who said getting her story right would be quite difficult, and that Miss de Mazia knew that biographies of Barnes and her would be "almost impossible for someone to get right." He did not tell me this to discourage me but I can say that with all I have discovered the aura and mystery that surrounds the nearly mythic Violette remains.

The Mantra and Her Legacy

When La Salle College honored Violette with an honorary doctorate on the 21st of October 1984—one of four she received in her lifetime—she accepted it with the "greatest gratitude…felt deeply and humbly." With brevity, she described the course of study she taught in the philosophy and appreciation of art at the Barnes. Seeing the importance of a work of art went beyond the boundaries of a frame. A work of art offered "cues and clues" to what could and should be the art of living. "Qualities that pertained to an intrinsic appeal to and a stimulation of the mind, an individuality, a link with the past, a seeding for the future, an expression of meanings and feelings of an individual's reactions to the world we are all given to live in, and a sharing of meanings and feelings with other human beings: every one of these features and still others that are concentrated in the work of the artist can, should, and would prevail in our daily living, and do prevail, if and when our daily living is to be—as it can, indeed, be—a work of art. That is the possibility that art affords to each one on earth —the possibility of making art and life kin."[178] This was her mantra and what motivated Violette as she taught her students, and as she penned her essays until the very last day of her life.

Her legacy is great. In addition to the four books she co-wrote with Dr Barnes, and the numerous *Vista* issues, Violette left twenty-nine essays. Most of which form the very structure of the curriculum at the Barnes Foundation to this day: "What to Look for in Art," "Learning to See," "Creative Distortion," "Expression," "The Decorative Aspect in Art," "Transferred Values," "Subject and Subject Matter," all introduce concepts to the student through analysis of the paintings within the collection. Students learn directly from the art itself; learning is not simply mimicking of a lecturer but an understanding of the concepts firsthand.

One can see easily that the Barnes' educational experiment that began with Dr. Barnes and John Dewey has remained exuberantly alive and well for nearly one-hundred years, and it is fair to say this is due significantly to Violette de Mazia's faith, loyalty, dedication, and brilliance as a lecturer, writer, and teacher. As for the tomorrows yet to be, this is how Ross Mitchell, the Director of Barnes-de Mazia Education and Outreach Programs at the Barnes Foundation, perceives the future of Violette's legacy:

"To make the program grow and evolve and be a living entity—that's the best way to do honor to her. Not a plaque, not even, frankly, you know, having her name on a lecture is all well and fine, but the true way of carrying on what her legacy is to make this class grow and live.

"There is so much going on at the Barnes with great positive possibilities to put the education front and center. I have been thinking about it from the perspective that Barnes and de Mazia were only able to take their mission so far—because Barnes' impatience and adversarial nature sabotaged the general acceptance of his ideals for art, democracy and education…and maybe he was just too far ahead of his time—and now is the perfect time to carry on their mission without the negative baggage. If we focus on everything good and positive in their mission the foundation would be the unique and vibrant institution that I believe that Barnes intended... We teach that art communicates what another person has seen, lived, and considered important so that the perceptive viewer can see the world through the painter's eyes. We accomplish this goal by teaching students to understand the unique language of the artist, without imposing our own interests, so that viewers can more completely understand what the painters have to say. We do this because to see the world from another person's perspective changes how we see our world, and through a shared learning experience, allowed by open and respectful dialogue, students better understand each other. With the end goal being that we grow more compassionate when we understand another person's point of view and society is more democratic the more its people understand the experiences of others...How's that for a lofty mission but that is what we teach!" [179]

Unique, very Barnesian and "Vio-brant" come to mind.

Epilogue

The journey began in Paris. It ended in Clarksboro, New Jersey at Eglington Cemetery on a grassy knoll sheltered by a century-old oak tree where Violette de Mazia is inurned. Here bronze plaques lie flush to the surface of the ground. They are not numerous, and are randomly placed. Even from a short distance they are barely seen. No tightly clustered nearly gothic rows of headstones surrounding this area, no paths paved with cement.

The manager of Eglington asked why I was writing a biography of Violette. This fine teacher who spent a lifetime at the Barnes Foundation would not have sought this attention, for she was modest. The only way one could really know her was by the way students spoke of her, and the many treasured letters they sent to her. She saved them all.

With directions to find Violette's resting place, even a flag on the knoll to mark the site, it is still impossible to find the precise location. For there is no bronze plaque to identify it, and this fills me with sadness. But then I begin to understand her purpose: It is here, on this canvas of rolling hills with its stone, soil, and pebble pathways where everything breathes in the light, space, and color that Violette merges with the composition, where she herself becomes part of an illuminating masterpiece. Such a masterpiece needs no title to be understood.

Acknowledgements

*B*eyond her sixty years at the Barnes Foundation as a teacher, director of education and trustee, much about Violette de Mazia's life has remained a mystery. There are tidbits about her in biographies of Dr. Albert C. Barnes, but beyond her contribution to *The Art in Painting, The French Primitives, The Art of Henri Matisse, The Art of Renoir, The Art of Cezanne*, and a handful of newspaper articles, little if anything is known about her or her friendship with students, and barely anything with accuracy about her life before she came to the United States and adopted Philadelphia as her home.

After several months of research at the Barnes Archives in Merion under the brilliant guidance of archivists Barbara Beaucar and Amanda McKnight, it was the author's good fortune to spend a year visiting the Violette de Mazia Archives in Wayne, Pennsylvania, before it was relocated to Barnes' Foundation new home on the Parkway in Philadelphia. Its director, Ross L. Mitchell, archivists Gregory McCoy, George Stradtman, and interns Elizabeth McDermott and Joanna Hurd skillfully guided my research through the entire collection. Poet and translator William T. Kulik assisted in the translation of the French in the treasure trove of love letters Violette received from her Egyptian fiancé. Those letters are a special insight into her life and the tragedy she experienced before leaving England for America.

Violette's history before crossing the Atlantic has come together dramatically through the talent and skill of genealogists Micheline Guttman in Paris, Jan Bousse in Belgium, Hazel Dakers in England, and Dr. Miri Shefer-Mossensohn, Chair of Middle Eastern and African History at Tele Aviv University.

Former Barnes students Peter Paone, Marilyn Bauman, Anita Gross, Rosalie Goldstein, Marcelle Pick, Bob and Sandy London, Eileen Serxner, Pearlann Gulden Horowitz, Irvin Nahan, Rina and Newton Malerman, Ellen Pyle Homsey, Margaret Pyle Hassert, Richard Segal, Gene Rochberg, Ross Lance Mitchell, Frank Colgan, Christina Czorpita, Elizabeth Cowitz (via her daughter Hannah Bar-Giora), Thomas Joseph Donleavy, Nicolas King, Elaine Heist, Sharon Bloomfield Hicks, Amy Weiner Sosnov, Hope Broker, Todd Makler, Sr., Todd Makler, Jr., Myrna Bloom Marcus, Jill Pomerantz, Renee Stern Zuritsky, Hope and Murray Seitchik generously shared their memories of Violette de Mazia and the Barnes Foundation. To all of them, and to this author, Violette de Mazia remains unforgettable.

Endnotes

1 Nathan Margolis and his wife, Adele, had been students at the Barnes.

2 Cimetière du Montparnasse, No 549, Division 25.

3 Cimetière du Montparnasse, No 549 Division 25.

4 The week of August 28th 1972, Violette was nominated by the French government to be Chevalier of Arts and Letters. *Main Line Chronicle*, August 31, 1972. [Clipping from Violette de Mazia Archives]. On December 2, 1973, there was "A Tribute To Violette de Mazia" at the Philadelphia Academy of Music Ballroom presented by The Friends of the Barnes Foundation to celebrate the appointment by France's Ministry of Cultural Affairs. "The de Mazia Quintet," by Bonnee Hoy, was written especially for the occasion. It was "conceived as a tightly structured work in cyclic form in which the sections of every movement interrelate with the sectional structure of all movements and ultimately all interrelate with the structure of the whole." Analysis by Bonnee Hoy, "A Tribute to Violette de Mazia," PCMC Encore Records, Philadelphia, PA 19117.

5 The Mazia family did not use the "de" in their name until after they immigrated to England. It was not on Violette's official birth record from the French National Archives. Levallois-Perret is located in the Hauts-de-Seine, a department of France that covers the western inner suburbs northwest of Paris. It is between Neuilly and Clichy just outside the perimeter of the city to the Northwest. The Upper Seine River rolls through this town historically known for two industries: The Eiffel Company, and Clément–Gladiator motorcars.

6   The Mazia family surname and given names vary in records. The surname appears varyingly as Mazia, Masia, and Massia. The honorific "de" does not appear in any records from France or Belgium. Sonny was born on March 21, 1865, the son of Aaron Micheliovitch Mazia. [Registers of Population, O 849/1990—O 1245/1900, Belgian Archives]. Sonny's occupation varies in records as well. In the *Almanach de commerce* 1912, S. Mazia: In Belgium, in later years, he is listed as an engineer. On his son Michel Georges Mazia's birth record dated March 17, 1894, Sonny declared himself to be the "directeur de la maison franco-suisse." The address of his mother and father in Paris was rue Saint Appoline 16. They were previously from Morteau, a little city in the Doubs river valley in Eastern France, near Switzerland. Aaron Micheliovitch Masia was born in Kamenetz; his wife, Olga Bolchover was born in Zaslav, February, 23, 1893.2.23, p.1.Violette's Parents' Marriage Record.Fraenkel-Masia.

7   In the 1896 Census, 49 rue Chaptal, Levallois-Perret, they were the fifth family listed. Source: Archives Town of Levallois-Perret, Archives Départementales des Hauts de Seine, Archives Municipales de Levallois-Perret, 26 Rue Clement-Bayard, 92300, Levallois-Perret, France. History of a house in Levallois-Perret, Project #8564, June 2015, Genealogists.com.

8   Sonny had a residence in the city of Brussels at boulevard du Hainaut 51 even before the rest of his family left Levallois-Perret. Sonny's parents, it seems, lived with Violette's family in Paris, Levallois-Perret, and in St. Gilles.

9   These included the Société royale Orphéique de Saint-Gilles, La Royale Réunion lyrique, Cercle Royal Offenbach, L'Offenbach Mère, L'Union Chorale, La Brabançonne, L'Écho du Fort, La Lyre Saint-Gilloise, L'Alauda, and Les Enfants du peuple.

10   Gustave Weyns was the owner. The street name changed to rue Emile Féron in 1920.

11   On his marriage license, Sonny is listed as a "comptable," an accountant. In the *Almanack*, he is listed as an "ingénieur," an engineer. There appears to be no explanation for the discrepancy.

12   Boys and girls attended this school, but their classes were separate. There was a boys' entrance at one end and a girls' entrance at the other. It was said that her brother never attended school, and was taught by a governess, but with a primary school on the very block where they lived (the same school as Violette would have attended but with separate entrances and classes for boys and girls), it seems logical that Georges could have begun his earliest schooling here. Records of these schools do not exist from that time, so it is impossible to ascertain when, where, and if, he actually attended.

13   Only 5.5 percent finished at the end of six years.

14   Known today at L'Athenee Royal Gatti De Gamond, the school celebrated its 150th year in 2014.

15   Certificate of Studies.

16   "Une récompense spéciale en accordée à: Mlle: Jeanne Mertens, Violette Mazia [sic, there was no "de" in her surname], Valérie Lamy." Gatti School Graduation Program, August 1914, p. 8. She turned 18 at the end of that month.

17   The former was launched in 1902, and the latter in 1897.

18   Bergen Steamship Company https://en.wikipedia.org/wiki/Bergen_Steamship_Company

19   The New York Times, November 1, 1914, Swears Belgians Were Massacred! Dr. Clement Philippe Describes Acts of Germans in Captured Villages, 200 Killed In Aerschot.

20   The first publicly listed residence for the Mazias in London, England, was in 1916 at 16 Boundary Road in St. John's Wood. By 1922, they were at 63 Fellows Road, near Primrose Hill and Regent's Park, in South Hampstead. Fanny moved from her Fellows Road home to one in Uxbridge/Ruislip during World War II. There was a compelling reason for the move. During the London Blitzkrieg, a single parachute mine had fallen on Fellows Road, several blocks from the de Mazia residence, and killed twenty-four people and destroyed six houses. Source: "The day lives were changed forever," Paul Keilthy, *Camden New Journal*, November 5, 2009, and republished on the Internet August 7, 2015. Vio-

lette's mother was a widow for sixteen years when she died in Ickenham, a village in Greater London. It was just a five-minute journey from her previous home.

21   London Private Schools, S25E, T25L London, EA 1921, Miss Barnett, 140 Alexandra Road, Boys and Girls, 66 total students.

22   1926.July 8.Jeannette Barnett To American Consul. Principal. Boarding SchoolDSCN1004. Jeanette Barnett's school was both a boarding and day school. It seemed to have a strong music curriculum. Two of their teachers, Emma Barnett the sister of the School Mistress, and Alison Temple, the governess, were Professors of Music.

23   C.E.Town, Secretary for Commercial Education and Assistant Secretary of the London Chamber of Commerce to Miss V. de Mazia. July 8, 1918. Also in *The Polytechnic Magazine*, September 1918, p.132. Her name is misspelled as Violette de Maiza.

24   Education, S. C. 2382, April 6, 1920. Pitman's School 152 Southampton Row, W.C. ED 15/23. Also, 4 W 1911.

25   Elie Catz to Violette de Mazia, May 20, 1920. Poem translated from the French by the author.

Si tu lisais, Violette, les secrets de mon âme
Et si tu connaissais mes sentiments pour toi,
Ton petit coeur chéri, ton doux coeur de femme
S'attendrirait peut-être et penserait à moi...

Si tu savais comme je voudrais te voir, chérie,
Te causer et te dire mon amour pour toi,
Tu entendrais peut-être ma pauvre voix meurtrie
Suppliante de crainte que tu ne l'écoutes pas....

Si tu savais, Viva, comme je désirerais
Que tu mes dises tes rêves ainsi que tes secrets
Que tu m'ouvres ton âme et me donnes ton coeur
Et que tu vives toujours dans l'eternal Bonheur

Ma belle petite Violette, douce comme l'aurore
Aux beaux yeux bleus d'azur et aux longs cheveux d'or

Cette voix qui t'implore la nuit comme le jour
C'est la voix de mon coeur, c'est la voix l'amour..."

26   March 1923, Soly Catz to Joe Catz. Postcard from Marseille. Port View. DSCN3767. How exactly Violette met the two brothers is unknown, but I conjecture that with her translation and stenography skills in English, German, French, Italian and Russian, she might have been hired by their father, who was an international agronomist with a need for someone skilled in multiple languages, able to translate letters to and from his multinational clients. Violette could possibly have met the brothers through this connection.

27   His parents were Nathan and Clementine Catz, second cousins of Romanian origin but Egyptian subjects. Joseph was educated in the French School Cairo and the College Scientifique, Lausanne, Switzerland. He also attended the University of London. During WWI, he served in the Zion Mule Corps, the forerunner of the Jewish Legion, and the Egyptian Labour Corps. He served in Dardanelles and Egypt. He became a naturalized British Citizen, having resided in London, England for three years, 1920 to 1923. He then joined the Royal Air Force.

28   July 21,1923, "Ma Petite Fiancee cherie," Joseph Catz to Violette de Mazia. Translated by the author. The SS *Mantua*, one of the P&O Line/British Indian Steam Navigation Company's steamships, sailed from London to Port Said. From there, Joe would travel by train to Cairo.

29   It seems that Violette's letters to Joe Catz no longer exist. Enough is described in his letters to infer her feelings, and those of her family.

30   His official British Passport indicates his date of birth as January 1, 1898. His parents, Nathan Itzhak Hacohen Catz and Clementine Shub, Egyptian subjects, were 2nd cousins of Roumanian origin. His siblings: Rose, Elie, Soly, Edith, Andre and Gaston.

31   Jabotinsky was a journalist, orator, Zionist leader who played a vital role in the establishment of the State of Israel. He wrote the memorial on the occasion of Joseph's death in a flight training accident in Abu Sueir, Egypt.

32 Patterson wrote *The Man-Eaters of Tsavo*, and was the model for Ernest Hemingway's character in "The Short Happy Life of Francis Macomber."

33 Joseph or Yosef Trumpeldor, an early Zionist activist and war hero. Vladimir (Ze'ev) Jabotinsky, Memorial to Joseph Katz, February 2, 1924. "Wounded twice, Joe remained in battle. The Zion Mule Corps bravely played a vital role at Gallipoli delivering water, and urgently needed ammunition. When they came under particularly heavy shellfire, many from the Mule Corps requested to join in the frontline fighting, but were denied because they could not be spared from the vital duties they were performing." General Hamilton wrote to General Maxwell on the 4th of May in 1915 from Cairo: "What we would have done without the Zion Mule Corps I do not know."

34 Certificate, "This is to certify that Lieut. J. Catz has been employed in this Brigade for the last 5 months," Captain A. S. Knight, Education Officer, Cairo Brigade, April 40, 1920.

35 "Absence is to love what fire is to the wind. It extinguishes the small, and revives the great." Translation by the author. The poem was sent by Joe Catz to Violette de Mazia from the *SS Mantua* in July 29, 1923. It has been attributed to Roger de Rabutin, the Comte de Bussy.

36 Ibid.

37 Ibid.

38 Ibid.

39 Joseph Catz to Violette de Mazia, Cairo, October 27, 1923.

40 Ibid.

41 Letter from Joseph Catz to Violette de Mazia, August 13, 1923. The Avro was a British fighter plane used as a trainer in World War I.

42 Tilbury Docks is London's major port. Joseph Catz to Violette de Mazia, October 28, 1923.

43 Ibid.

44 Letter from Joseph Catz to Violette de Mazia, Abu Sueir, October 29, 1923. Violette de Mazia Foundation Archives.

45 Ibid.

46 Ibid.

47 Letter from Joseph Catz to Violette de Mazia, Abu Sueir, October 31, 1923. Violette de Mazia Foundation.

48 Ibid.

49 Ibid.

50 Ibid.

51 Ibid. The underlining is Joe's emphasis.

52 Letter from Joe Catz to Violette de Mazia, Abu Sueir, November 8, 1923.

53 Letter from Joe Catz to Violette de Mazia, November 8, 1923.

54 Letter from Joe Catz to Violette de Mazia, November 12, 1923.

55 Ibid.

56 Royal Air Force fatalities for 1923.

57 Letter from Joe Catz to Rose Catz, Abu Sueir, November 15, 1923.

58 Ibid.

59 Ibid.

60 Letter from Joe Catz to Violette de Mazia, November 13, 1923.

61 Ibid.

62 Letter from Rose Catz to Joe Catz, November 12, 1923.

63 Ibid.

64 Ibid.

65 Letter from Joe Catz to Violette de Mazia, Friday, November 16, 1923.

66   Letter from Joe Catz to Violette de Mazia, November 19, 1923.

67   Letter from Joe Catz to Violette de Mazia, November 22, 1923.

68   Letter from Joe Catz to Violette de Mazia, November 19, 1923.

69   Ibid.

70   Letter from Joe Catz to Violette de Mazia, November 29, 1923 and November 30, 1923.

71   Letter from Joe Catz to Violette de Mazia, December 3, 1923 and continuation of letter from November 30, 1923.

72   Ibid.

73   Violette de Mazia, Number 321, November 23, 1923, "Three Wonderful Solos."

74   Letter from Joe Catz to Violette, December 4, 1923.

75   Ibid.

76   Letter from Joe Catz to Violette, December 4, 1923. To my knowledge, no letters from Violette to Joe Catz have survived.

77   Ibid.

78   Joe explained at the foot of his letter that a "do" was an Air Force slang expression meaning a "'show' or 'exploit' or anything to that effect."

79   Letter from Joe Catz to Violette, December 6, 1923.

80   Letter from Joe Catz to Violette, December 10, 1923.

81   Letter from Joe to Violette, December 11, 1923.

82   Letter from Joe to Violette, December 12, 1923.

83   Letter from Joe to Violette, December 15, 1923.

84   Ibid.

85   RAF Record, Joe's Death.

86   1923.Catz_casualty report (1), A.M. Form 470, Royal Air Force Casualty Card, CATZ P/O [Pilot Officer], Regiment: RAF, Unit No.4

F.T.S., Official Records Noted 27-2-24. The cause of his death was a fracture at the back of his skull, for which there is a very high fatality rate. He died in the Military Hospital in Ismailia, about 22 miles from Abù Sueir, two weeks short of his 26th birthday. Two death records: 1923.12.17. Certified Copy of Death, SA083748. General Register Office England. Military record: An Entry in the Army Register Book of Births, Deaths and Marriages. Certified Copy of An Entry of Death, SA 083748, Application Number 519891/1.

87   *The Sphinx*, December 22, 1923, p.14.

88   Ibid.

89   "Un Chevalier Juif," *L'Aurore, Journal d'information Juives*," December 19, 1924, p. 3.

90   Ibid.

91   The Bayuks lived at 2319 N. Broad Street, literally next door to the Sephardic temple known as Mikveh Israel Synagogue. The Bayuks, however, do not seem to have been members of this synagogue.

92   *Aquitania*, Cunard Line, from Southampton to New York, May 17, 1924. On the ship manifest, her age is given as 24 years and 8 months. The travel visa is the only time she estimates more accurately the actual year of her birth in a public record. The correct date of birth, as mentioned above, was August 30, 1896.

93   Rosalie Silverman Goldstein Interview, May 23, 2016.

94   N. E. Mullen to Miss Violette De (sic) Mazia, September 11, 1925. "We inquired of the Bryant Teachers' Agency for a teacher of French and your name was given to us." Nelle E. Mullin to Violette. September 11, 1925.

95   At about the same time, Jeannette Portenar responded to a Barnes advertisement for stenographer and bookkeeper. Portenar held a BS degree in Education from the University of Pennsylvania, but when she tried to get a job in the public schools, she found it impossible because she was Jewish. This is the reason she gave to Dr. Barnes. Barnes never mentioned that Violette was Jewish. She may not have told him; at least, early on.

96   Op. Cit. Nelle E. Mullin to Vio.Bryant Teachers' Agency, September 11, 1925. N. E. Mullen to Violette de Mazia, September 11, 1925. Just a few years later, 1928, Thomas Munro would publish his seminal work, *Scientific Method in Aesthetics.*"

97   Barnes Foundation Archives, Violette de Mazia to Albert C. Barnes, July 4, 1926, AR.ABC.1926.214. Translated by the author: "Cher Docteur, Il est parait-il, fatal que je vous dérange chaque fois á la veille de votre voyage. Par contre, j'ai toujours la bonne chance que vous ne partez pas un jour plus tôt que le jour de votre départ…En termes plus clairs: j'ai fait la demande pour le "quota" et le Consul Amèricain a londres me demande entre autres documents a présenter, "a lettre from a person in authority or of good standing (American citizen, but no relative) who knows me well and can establish my character."J'espère que vous vous reconnaitrez bien sous la qualification sus-mentionnée et que vous aurez la grande amabilité de m'envoyer une telle letter a remettre au Consul—ce qui m'aiderait a franchir le Rubicon. Mon grand merci à l'avance. Au sujet du but de mon voyage, je déclarerai que c'est pour "study and teach."Hier, je vous ai adressé le catalogue des Francais modernes de la Tate Gallery. J'y ai retrouvé "les Parapluies" de Renoir. Ils ont aussi de lui un portrait d'une femme, d'un effet tout bleu; de très beaux Daumiers, Manets, Degas. Dans "la Baignade" de Seurat, je n'ai pas trouvé de pointillisme tel que je le concevais. Ensemble assez significatifs, mais une maigre représentation de Cézanne.—Enfin, cette vision a rafraîchi en moi des réminiscences. "Fondamentales" plus interesantes qui m'ont aidée à classifier mes idées.
   Il me reste encore à vous souhaiter un heureux voyage de retour et d'emporter avec vous une collection de souvenirs choisis."

98   Opening Exhibition of the Modern Foreign Gallery, June 8 to October 9, 1926.

99   The recommended reading list was entitled "A First Requisite In Art Education." These books are listed in the May 1925 issue of *The Journal of the Barnes Foundation*, p. 33. Among those on this list were books by Bosanquet, Dewey, Ellis, McDougall, Santayana, Trotter, Buermeyer, Barnes, and Mullen.

100 For example, her definition of an artist as "a person who can express his experience (forms) in a suitable material so that they will arouse similar feelings in the observer...not an exact copy of the object that aroused the artist's emotion; in fact what makes the artist a creator is his ability to rearrange his experiences into new and more meaningful forms—that is, he puts on canvas certain aspects of nature, as he conceives them by the use of his imagination."

101   Mary Mullen, p. 28.

102   Violette's departure date from Cherbourg, France in August 1939— more than a decade after leaving England—and near the outbreak of World War II mirrors her and her family's dramatic departure from Belgium in August 1914 at the brink of World War I.

103   Albert C. Barnes to Girls, July 9, 1927, On Board *SS Berengaria*, "A Propos du early Germans."

104   This was two years before the first edition of *The Art of Henri Matisse* was published by the Barnes Foundation Press. "Cryptic" probably refers to Violette's habit of interspersing Pitman shorthand and ideograms along with longhand writing when she took notes. Her stenographer notebooks are filled with them, and need considerable deciphering to understand them. 80.1931.3.31.Albert C. Barnes to Jack (John Dewey]. Miss de Mazia's notes on Matisse's big *Joie de Vivre*. 1931, JohnDewey. AR.ABC.1931.173

105   Nice 11 Fevrier 1933. "Chére Madmoiselle, Ne pouvant trouver un traducteur ayant l'intelligence des idées, je ne veux pas attendu plus longtemps pour vous oui combien je suis touché de l'effort énorme que vous et le Dr. Barnes avez accompli pour ecrire n? mon oeuvre un livre aussi le lieux—C'est un véritable document. Je ne puis malheureusement aujourd hui que juger de sa presentation qui est excellente—J'espere avoir bientôt le plaisir de vous renouveler mes compliments d'une façon plus précise un attendant agrée chez mademoiselle, mes vifs remerciements et mes hommages respectueux. Henri Matisse. Translation by the author.

106   September 6, 1926, United States Lines, 6.1926.9.6.Mary Mullen to Violette de Mazia.p.1.DSCN2275. For several years, from 1928 to 1932, Geiger was Violette's travel companion in Europe.

107 68.1927.7.5 (July 5) Hotel Subasio. Assisi. Violette to Jane Geiger. The Papers of Violette de Mazia.

108 VDM Notes, Jan Vermeer Notes, Mauritzhaus, Hague, Holland, June 7, 1927.

109 *Three Lectures on Aesthetics*, Bernard Bosanquet, 1915, London: MacMillan and Co.

110 2014-07-09 23.20.32. Jan Vermeer—1632–1675. No. 670. "Girl with Turban" ("Girl with a Pearl"). Violette de Mazia Notes.

111 *V.d.M Notes, Dutch, Flemish, French, Miscellaneous* notebook: 2014-07-09 23.20.38, Jan Vermeer, #92, View of Delft, Hague, June 7, 1927. Barnes Archives.

112 Frances Pepente Wright, "Barnes in Merion," May 25, 1977. Myrna Bloom Marcus kindly shared this poem that was sent to her by Wright.

113 Ellen Homsey, Associate Editor, *The Barnes Foundation Journal of the Art Department*, Vol. III, Autumn, 1972, No. 2, Tributes.

114 Violette did not publish until the 1970s, There was a gap of more than twenty years after Barnes' fatal accident before turning her lecture notes into polished essays. Eleanor Pyle Homsey, a student of hers at the Barnes, was key to this creative and productive period. Her contribution as Violette's associate editor cannot be overestimated.

115 Two of Munro's essays appear in issues one and two of the first volume of the Journal of the Barnes Foundation: *A Constructive Program For Teaching Art.*

116 Impressions Of Class Thomas Munro, 31.1927.3.21, 2 of 2, AR.ABC.1927.380. Barnes Foundation Archives.

117 Ibid.

118 Ibid.

119 Ibid.

120 Ibid.

121   The Barnes Foundation: Reality vs. Myth, Gilbert M. Cantor, p. 62.

122   Among the dedicatory speakers were officials from the University of Pennsylvania and Colombia University, a Montgomery County judge, and a State Senator who was also a resident of Merion. *Dr. Barnes of Merion, A Biography*, Henry Hart, 1963, p. 97.

123   Barnes Foundation Archives, Bryant Teachers Agency, 1925, AR.ABC.1925.104.

124   Ross Lance Mitchell Interview, May 1, 2015. Director of Barnes-de Mazia Education and Outreach Programs at The Barnes Foundation, and Former Director of the Violette de Mazia Foundation.

125   Matisse and Strawinsky, a chapter in *The Art of Henri Matisse*, Albert C. Barnes and Violette de Mazia.

126   Translated from the French by the author. September 17, 1926. *M'isoler! Je jouis à l'avance de cette perspective de solitude pendent laquelle chaque minute sera remplie de visions et de révisions dont ma mémoire a* été si *agréablement chargée. Il me semble que j'ai complètement perdu la faculté de m'ennuyer—ce que je considère, naturellement—comme une rare et précieuse acquisition. Je sais à qui je suis redevable de ce "nouveau monde" dans lequel je vis à présent, et je ne viens pas vous remercier et mettre un point, car je sens que je vous serai reconnaissante toujours sans jamais y mettre de point. Mes parents ne se réjouissent pas trop de mon nouveau départ, d'autant plus que j'ai passé très peu de temps avec eux, et si je ne jamais tant l'Amérique, et si le monde n'y* était *si bon, je ne me serais pas donné la peine de lui* être *aussi désagréable que de revenir si vite.*

127   Interview Ross L. Mitchell, May 1, 2015. When Ross L. Mitchell was working at the Barnes Foundation, Julia was still there. "It was in the trust indenture that she would have a lifetime position and free housing and pay and she was still there."

128   1927, *Les Arts a Paris*, La Peinture, Violette de Mazia. Translated from the French by the author.

129   Art and Education, "Learning to See," p. 148.

130 Bob London to Gilbert Cantor. 12.11.1961.DSCN2922

131 Richard Segal, conversation, January 29, 2015.

132 Barnes Foundation Archives, Education Writings, *The French Primitives*, Box 5, Background Materials. AR.EDUC.WR.FP.19, p. 199.

133 Note 3. Paris, Louvre, July 2, 1929, Attribué (sic, French for attributed) a Francois Clouet, No. 133B *Jean Babou, Seigneur de la Bourdaisiere*. Barnes Foundation Archives, 1929–1930 Education Writings The French Primitives. Box 3 Background materials AR.ED.WR.FP.14. The Barnes Foundation Archives-Travel notes in typescript, carbon copy and manuscript form. Pt. 1.

134 *The French Primitives*, Box 5, Note 12, Florence Uffizi, July 9, 1929. Froment Niccola of Avignon, No 1065, Resurrection of Lazarus.

135 Barnes Foundation Archives, Education Writings, *The French Primitives*, Box 5, Background Materials. AR.EDUC.WR.FP.19, Color Relations, p. 12,

136 Violette is referring to the frescoes in the 13th century Ferrand Tower in Pernes-les-Fontaines, a town south of Carpentras in the Vaucluse department of Provence.

137 According to Henry Hart, in *Dr. Barnes of Merion*, p. 128, the detailed analyses of Matisse's paintings in the Barnes publication were co-written by Dr. Barnes and Violette. After Violette researched and analyzed the works of art, Barnes responded with his reactions to her findings. English was probably the fourth or fifth language she mastered—after French, Italian, German, and possibly even Dutch. Her mastery of spoken English was exceptional. I recall her lengthy lectures at the Barnes fluently delivered. She had an exceptional command of the English language, and was never at a loss for words. This is what I recall from her lectures in 1963. However, I do not doubt that the book was a group process.

138 This includes all the groups for Monday, Tuesday, Wednesday and Thursday classes and seminars. The total numbers of students grew over the years. "From 1950 on, we have enrolled more than seventy students each year in our course. The number has increased each year. In the

school year 1960–1961, seventy-four students were admitted in the first-year group alone, and the total enrollment in the course was one-hundred and thirty-one. For the school-year (1963–1964) one hundred and sixty-two students were enrolled in the course. For the '64–'65 school-year, 191 were enrolled." Court Case Files, p. 7. Paragraph 1. Top of second column."2014-08-13 21.39.55.

139 Anita Gross Interview.

140 Based on Rachel Sterrenberg's vocal Analysis of Violette de Mazia from a Dictabelt recording of Violette's, December 23rd and 24th, 2014.

141 Ibid.

142 Ibid.

143 Violette Orientation Transcription. Dictabelt Arhive 1 of 5, c. 1970s.

144 Chris Callahan was Violette's assistant for approximately four years. He was hired in December of 1973.

145 Vio's notes student interviews.1971.1973.1974.1976.1986

146 Ibid.

147 Interview with Richard Segal, March 5, 2014. Segal was a stand-in for Violette in her last years, on the rare times she was too ill to teach. She was already in her nineties by then.

148 "From 1950 on, we have enrolled more than seventy students each year in our course. The number has increased each year. In the school-year 1960–1961 seventy-four students were admitted in the first-group alone, and the total enrollment in the course was one-hundred and thirty-one. For the current school-year (1963–1964) one hundred and sixty-two students were enrolled in the course. For the '63–'65 school-ear, 191 were enrolled." Court Selected Cases, 2014-08-13 21.39.55, p. 7, para. 5. Miss de Mazia's comments re Lois Forer.

149 Interview with Hope and Murray Seitchik, October 27, 2014.

150 May 18, 1937, Samuel B. Hadden, M.D. to A.C. Barnes, 1937 Barnes Foundation Archives, AR.ABC.1937.318 .

151   104.1960.5.28.Richard J. Wattenmaker to Miss de Mazia, Sidney Frick File 2 of 5. Administration Central File, Correspondence: AR.CFC.1960.461.

152   Ibid.

153   Eileen Serxner Interview, January 27, 2014.

154   Ibid.

155   Nicholas King, artist in residence at the Barnes, who assisted de Mazia in the galleries.

156   Eileen Serxner Interview, January 27, 2014.

157   Irvin Nahan Interview, January 30, 2014.

158   Barton Church, "Girl in a Chair," oil on canvas, 1951.

159   Nahan meant "sensuous," in the aesthetic sense, as well as implying she was comfortable in her own body.

160   Nahan interview.

161   The Cezanne painting that I recall Violette using for this "performance" was the Card Players in the main gallery; for Rina, it was a Cezanne landscape. Beethoven's Fifth Symphony was appropriate for either one. Repetition in a major key is central to both.

162   Richard Segal and Ellen Pyle Homsey interview.

163   V-O is Vio (Barnes' nickname for Violette) and L-N for Ellen Pyle Homsey. It was through her sister, Margaret Pyle Hassert, a talented writer and editor in her own right, that I learned the meaning of the acronym.

164   Margaret and Ellen are the granddaughters of the well-known artist Ellen Bernard Thompson Pyle, an illustrator of a multitude of covers for *The Saturday Evening Post* and other publications.

165   Richard Segal interview, January 29, 2015.

166   One observation of Homsey's is a surprise. When I mention the Japanese feast that Newt Malerman's prepared for Violette in which she was able to identify just about every spice used, she countered that it was

contrary to the way Violette ate when she sent her out to shop for her. "She ate the same thing every day and she liked it in just one way. It was very simple. It wasn't twenty different flavors...." She loved delicatessen, the rare beef from Hymie's, which was easily accessible, and she craved chocolate sandwiches made with French bread. Violette had a skilled palate that could easily identify the subtlest of seasonings, but in everyday life she seemed to court simplicity and repetition. Toasted chocolate sandwiches may have brought back pleasant childhood memories of the lunches made for her when they lived in Belgium and England. Hymie's cold cuts were probably the closest Violette could get to French and Belgian charcuterie at that time in the neighborhood of Lower Merion.

167   Ellen Pyle Homsey and Richard Segal Interview, March 5, 2014.

168   Violette may have actually been hypersensitive to certain colors, and perhaps why she wore tinted spectacles.

169   She had knowledge of Yiddish, but I do not know if she was fluent in that language.

170   March 7, 1960 to be precise. Her name on the death certificate is Mildred C. Evans, age 58. She had probably remarried, and was no longer known as Mrs. Winnings. (Kerns-Winnings death certificate)

171   Christies Auctions. Violette de Mazia Art & Property Sold at Auctions.

172   "The Mullen Collection," Important Paintings from the Estate of Nelle E. Mullen, Merion, Pennsylvania, Wednesday, November 15, Samuel F. Freeman & Co, 1967.

173   Sharon Bloomfield Hicks Interview, October 22, 2014. "I knew her for 18 months, basically, 18, or 19 months."

174   Ibid. Sharon Bloomfield Hicks Interview.

175   Medical Log, Dr. Cornman prescribed Elixir Terpin hydrate, Cerose cough medicine, Hycodan, Robitussin.

176   Medical Log, K. Phillips, July 16, 1988. Commonwealth of Pennsylvania, Certificate of Death, Violette de Mazia, 7479012, June 27, 2013. Dr. Cornman listed chronic obstructive pulmonary disease, renal

failure, hyperkalemia, and diabetes as conditions contributing to her death; atherosclerotic vascular disease for 30 years, mitral heart disease for 20; and cardiac failure as the immediate cause of death. Dr. Cornman wrote the final entry in the medical log: "After a long & valiant struggle against an incurable condition Miss de Mazia, who had spent a life working for other people accepted the inevitable and with dignity and a minimum of trouble to other people left this life for the greater one to come at 2:35 P.M. on 9/20/88."

177   Dorothy Antley, the night nurse.

178   Violette de Mazia, "Aspect of art that engrosses me," speech for her LaSalle doctorate.

179   Ross L. Mitchell, Interview, November 18, 2015.

Index

A

Art and Education. See "Learning to See"
Art Appreciation course, 57–61, 92–93, 96, 108
Art in Painting, The, 46, 73, 78, 81
Art of Cezanne, 48
Art of Renoir, 48
Art of Henri Matisse, The, 47–48, notes 104, 125

B

Barnes, Albert C. Dr., 3, 47–48, 54–59, 62–64, 73, 86, 91, 93, 96, 99, 104–107, 109, notes 95, 105, 122, 137,. *See also The Art in Painting*
Barnes connection to Violette, 45–48, 54, 56, 58–69, 85
Barnes Foundation, 1–2, 44–45, 47, 55–57, 71, 78, 83, 91, 93, 95, 99, 100, 103, 109, 111–113, notes 4, 97, 99, 104, 115, 116, 121, 123, 124, 127, 132, 133, 135, 150
Barnes school, 3, 16, 44–45, 53–59, 62–63, 65, 76–78, 80–83, 86–88, 91, 93–94, 99–100, 107–108, notes 1, 114, 133, 155
Bayuk, Samuel (uncle of Violette) and family, 42–44, note 91
Belgium and the Mazia family, 9–10, 13, 42, 106, notes 6, 102, 166
Birth, 9
Bryant Teacher's Agency, 44–45, 57, notes 96, 123
Buermeyer, Lawrence, 46, 54, 63, note 99

C

Card Players, The, 2, 68, 91, note 161. *See also* Violette conducting to art.

132

Catz, Elie, 17–19, note 25
Catz, Joseph (Joe), 19–43. *See also* Mazia, Sonny, resistance to Joe Catz; Jabotinsky, Vladimir
  as fighter pilot, 20, 23, 30–33, 35–40
  and Gallipoli, 19–20
  death, 40–41, 43
  in Cairo, 17, 19, 21, 24–29, 30–42
Church, Barton, 85–86, 94, note 158
Cimetière du Montparnasse, 5, notes 2–3
"Creative Distortion" 109

D

"Decorative Aspect in Art, The," 109
Dewy, John, 45–48, 54–56, 59, 63, 103, 109, notes 99, 104

E

Eglington Cemetery, 111
Ensembles in art, 78
Europe art trips, 48–54, 68–69, 92
"Expression," 109

F

Forme plastique, 60–61
French tutor, 44–45
Fraenkel family, 5–7, 106, note 6
French Primitives, The, 56, 65, 74, 112, notes 132, 133, 134, 135, 139

G

Ghent Altarpiece, 64
Girl in a Chair, 86
Girl with Turban, 50
Goldstein, Rosalie Silverman (French student), 43, 112, note 93
Gross, Anita, 113, note 139

H

Hart, Henry, note 122, 137
Hicks, Sharon Bloomfield, 100–105, 113, note 173

Homsey, Ellen Pyle (associate editor *Vista*), 92–93, 95, 97, 102, 109, 113, notes 113, 114, 162–163, 166–167

I

Interviewing students, 70–71, 76, 80–82, 100, note 139
Introductory lecture, 73, 70, 76–80, 109

J

Jabotinsky, Vladimir, 19–20, 28, 39, notes 31, 33
Jean Babou, Seignor de la Bourdaisiere, 64, note 133
Jewish, 5, 17, 19, 28, 40–41
Joie de Vivre (The Joy of Life) (Matisse), 48, note 104
Journal of the Barnes Foundation, 55, notes 99, 115

K

L

La Baignade, 45, note 97
La Salle College, 108
Latches Lane, 1, 3
"Learning to See," in *Art and Education*, 48, 81, 109, note 129
Leda, and the Swan, 2
"Le Peinture," *Les Arts a Paris*, 59, note 128
Les Parapluies (Tate), 45, note 97
London, Bob, 62, 107, 113, note 130
London (city), vi, 15–18, 21, 24, 28, 33–34, 37–38, 42–45, 58, 95, 106, notes 20, 23, 27–28, 42

M

Makler, Paul, Jr. (Todd), 77, 113
Makler, Todd, Sr., 77, 113
Malerman, Rina, 88–90, 113
Malerman, Newt, 88–91, 113, note 166
Marcus, Myrna Bloom, 53–54, 113, note 112
Matisse, Henri. *See also Art of Henri Matisse, The* Letter to Violette, translation from French to English by author, 47, note 104
Mazia, Feige (Fanny) Fraenkel (mother), 7, 9–10, 26, 106, note 20

Mazia, Sonny (father), 7–10, 23, 25–29, 36, 42, notes 6, 8, 11
  resistance to Joe Catz, 23, 25–26, 28–29, 33
Mise au Tombeau, 64
Mitchell, Ross L. (Director of Barnes-de Mazia Education and Outreach Programs at the Barnes Foundation), 57, 109, 112–113, notes 124, 127, 179
Mullen, Nelle and Mary, 44, 46–48, 54, 63, 95, 99, notes 94, 96, 99, 101, 106, 172, 141
Munro, Thomas (Violette's teacher), 45, 54–56. 59, notes 96, 115–116
Music Lesson, The, 55

N

Nabokoff, Nicolas, 54
Nahan, Irvin, 85–87, 113, notes 157, 159, 160

O

Outfits for art classes, Violette's, 84

P

Paone, Peter, 3–4, 113
Pinto, Angelo, 63

Q

R

Resurrection of Lazarus, 64, note 134

S

Schools
  as student, 10–12, 15–17, 19–21, 46
  as teacher, 47–48, 54, 70–81
Segal, Richard, 76, 91–94, 102–103, 113, notes 131, 147, 162, 165, 167
Seitchik, Hope and Murray, 78, 80, 113, note 149
Serxner, Eileen, 83–85, 113, notes 153, 1567
Sterrenberg, Rachel, 67–69, note 140. *See also* Voice
"Subject and Subject Matter," 109

T

"Transferred Values," 109
Tyler School of Fine Arts, 81, 88–89, 100

U

University of Pennsylvania, 45, 62, 81–82, notes 95, 122

V

View of Delft, 50–51, note 111
Violette "conducting" to art, 68, 91, endnote 161
Voice, 67–69. *See also* Sterrenberg, Rachel
VOLN Press, 92. *See also* Homsey, Ellen Pyle

W

Wattenmaker, Richard, 82–83, note 151
"What to Look for in Art,"109
Wright, Frances Pepente, 53–54, note 112

X

Y

Z

Zion Mule Corps, 19–20, 39, notes 27, 33